CW00927384

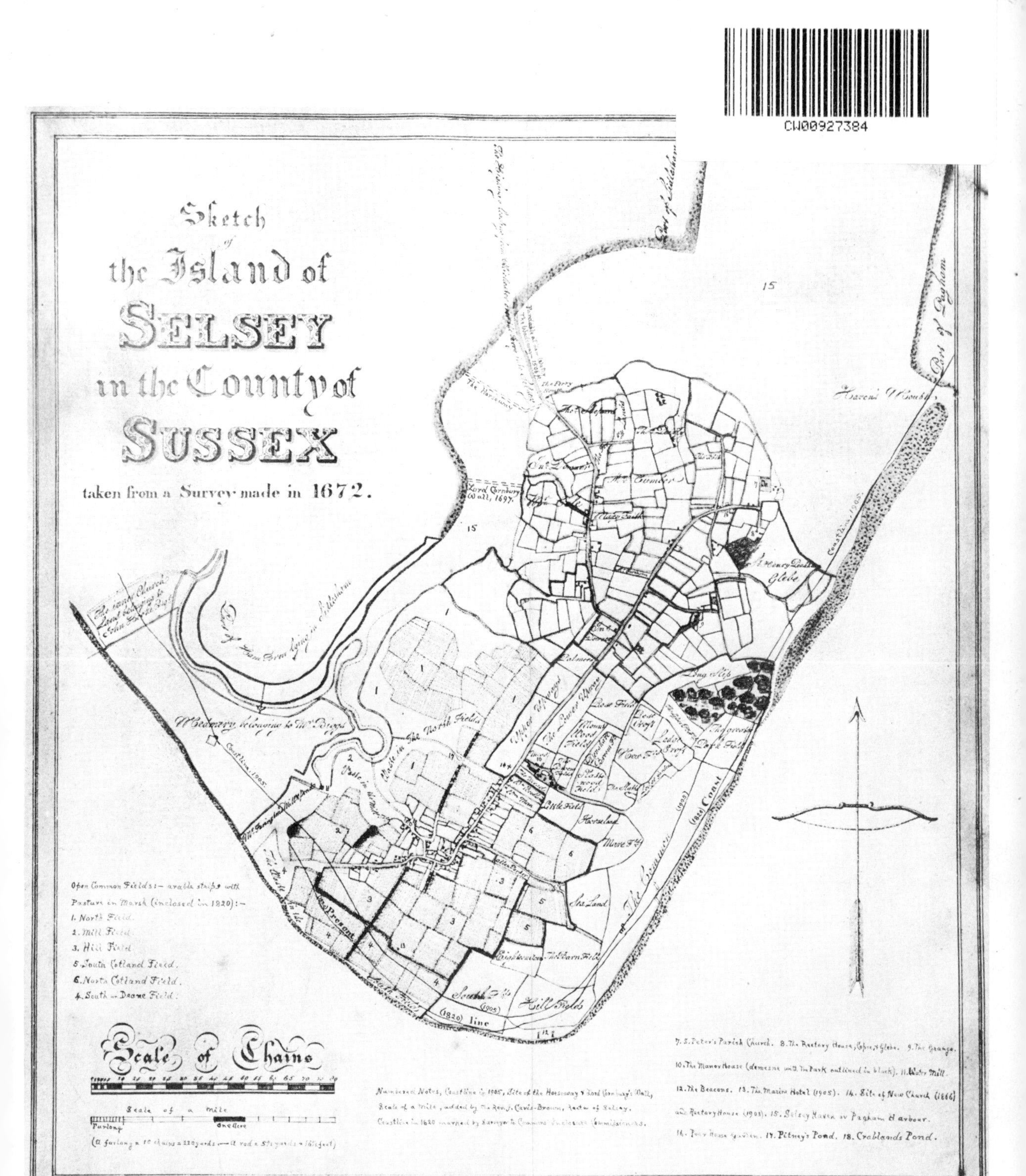

Map of the 'Island' of Selsey drawn in 1672, on which the coastlines of 1820 and 1905 have been added later.

A History of
SELSEY

Aerial view of the Selsey peninsula, taken in 1959. Many prominent features can be picked out including the lifeboat station, the sea defences and groynes, Broadreeds holiday camp near the Bill and the line of the old tramway near the golf course at the top of the picture.

A History of
SELSEY

Frances Mee

Phillimore

1988

Published by
PHILLIMORE & CO. LTD.
Shopwyke Hall, Chichester, Sussex

© Frances Mee, 1988

ISBN 0 85033 672 4

Printed and bound in Great Britain by
RICHARD CLAY LTD.
Chichester, Sussex

For Derek
Thanks for everything

Contents

List of Illustrations

I would like to express sincere thanks to the following for permission to reproduce illustrations: Jon Wynne-Tyson, Frontispiece, 1, 2, 3, 7, 8, 10, 13, 14, 15, 18, 19, 20, 21, 23, 24, 25, 26, 27, 29, 30, 31a, 32, 33, 34, 35, 36, 37, 38, 41, 42, 43, 54, 55, 56, 57a, 58, 59, 60, 61, 62, 63, 64, 67, 68, 69, 72, 73, 74, 76, 78, 79, 80, 81, 82, 83, 84, 85, 86, 87, 91, 92a, 93, 94, 96, 97, 98, 100, 103a, 104, 105, 106 and 108; West Sussex County Library Service, 12, 28, 52 and 88; Derek Mee, 16, 44, 66, 75, 77 and 99; Mr. R. Carbines, 39; Trinity House, London, 40; Peter Ogden, 45, 65, 69 and 89; Mrs. Gertrude Brown, 50; Clifford Fidler, 53; the Selsey Golf Club, 71; Mrs. M. Williamson, 90a; Barclays Bank PLC, 101 and 102; Mrs. M. Tupper, 103b; Selsey Football Club, 107; Stevens Estate Agents, street map of Selsey.

Acknowledgements

This book could never have been written without the help and advice of many people and I wish to record my heartfelt thanks to all who have played any part, however large or small. Writing this book has restored my waning faith in humanity – I now realise that there is a vast store of goodwill and helpfulness in a village like Selsey, just waiting to be tapped. I very rarely met with a closed door when I made requests for assistance and was usually greeted with friendliness, enthusiasm and a genuine desire to help.

I wish to thank three people in particular: Jon Wynne-Tyson who first inspired me to write this book and has given me help and encouragement ever since; Clifford Fidler who has shown endless patience in answering countless questions, some trivial and some profound, and whose knowledge of local people and places has made my work so much easier; and Patrick Moore, who graciously agreed to write the Foreword for this book. I am also grateful to all those people who gave up time to talk to me about various aspects of Selsey, past and present, or who took the trouble to send me information by post: Mr. John Allpress, Mr. B. J. Arrow, Mrs. J. Bowyer, Mr. D. Brooks, Mr. Harold Brown, Mr. R. Carbines, Rev. V. R. Cassam, Mr. C. Cockayne, Mr. C. H. E. Cox, Very Rev. Canon P. J. Cox, J. G. Craven, the Department of the Environment, Mr. Alec Down, Rev. F. R. Dowson, Mr. A. Eames, Dr. J. Fines, Mr. M. Goodchild; Mr. M. S. Jukes, Mr. & Mrs. R. Lewendon, Mr. V. Littleboy, Mr. T. T. J. McCarthy, Mr. F. W. J. Morris, Mrs. L. Nash, Mrs. Meg Nelson, Mr. Peter Ogden, Mr. N. D. Orchard, Post Office Archives (London), Mrs. Natalie Richards, Mr. G. H. R. Rounce, Mr. N. M. Shouls, Mr. & Mrs. N. Slack, Trinity House Information Office (London), Mr. & Mrs. J. Tupper, Weald and Downland Open Air Museum.

I am very grateful to Mrs. Patricia Gill, County Archivist, and all her staff at the Record Office in Chichester, and the staff in the reference departments at the Chichester and Bognor Regis Libraries.

I must also express my thanks to Mr. Philip Harris, Managing Director of Phillimore & Co., for his willingness to back me in this venture, and to Mr. Noel Osborne, Editorial Director of Phillimore, for his advice and guidance.

These acknowledgements would not be complete without a mention of my husband Derek who has shown great understanding when I have neglected housework and gardening to concentrate on a project which became something of an obsession, and whose encouragement kept me going when times got hard.

Foreword

Many people – certainly all sailors – have heard of Selsey Bill, but how many people know much about the village of Selsey itself? It is somewhat off the beaten track. There is only one road down to it from Chichester, so that nobody can drive through it from place A to place B – a fact which is a source of considerable satisfaction to those who live there. It is not large; it is not a village of what is so often termed 'outstanding natural beauty'; and its sands are not to be compared with those of Bognor which, despite the somewhat unflattering remarks by King George V, has the best beach on the south coast.

Yet Selsey has unique charm. There is something about its 'atmosphere' which cannot be duplicated elsewhere. It is a friendly place with a long history; records of it go back far into the past, and in every sphere it can provide a great deal of interest. Today it is a village which is very much alive, and very well aware of its traditions. Not for many years has it been the subject of a detailed study. Read this new book by Frances Mee, and I hope you will appreciate that Selsey is something very much more than just another Sussex village.

Patrick Moore

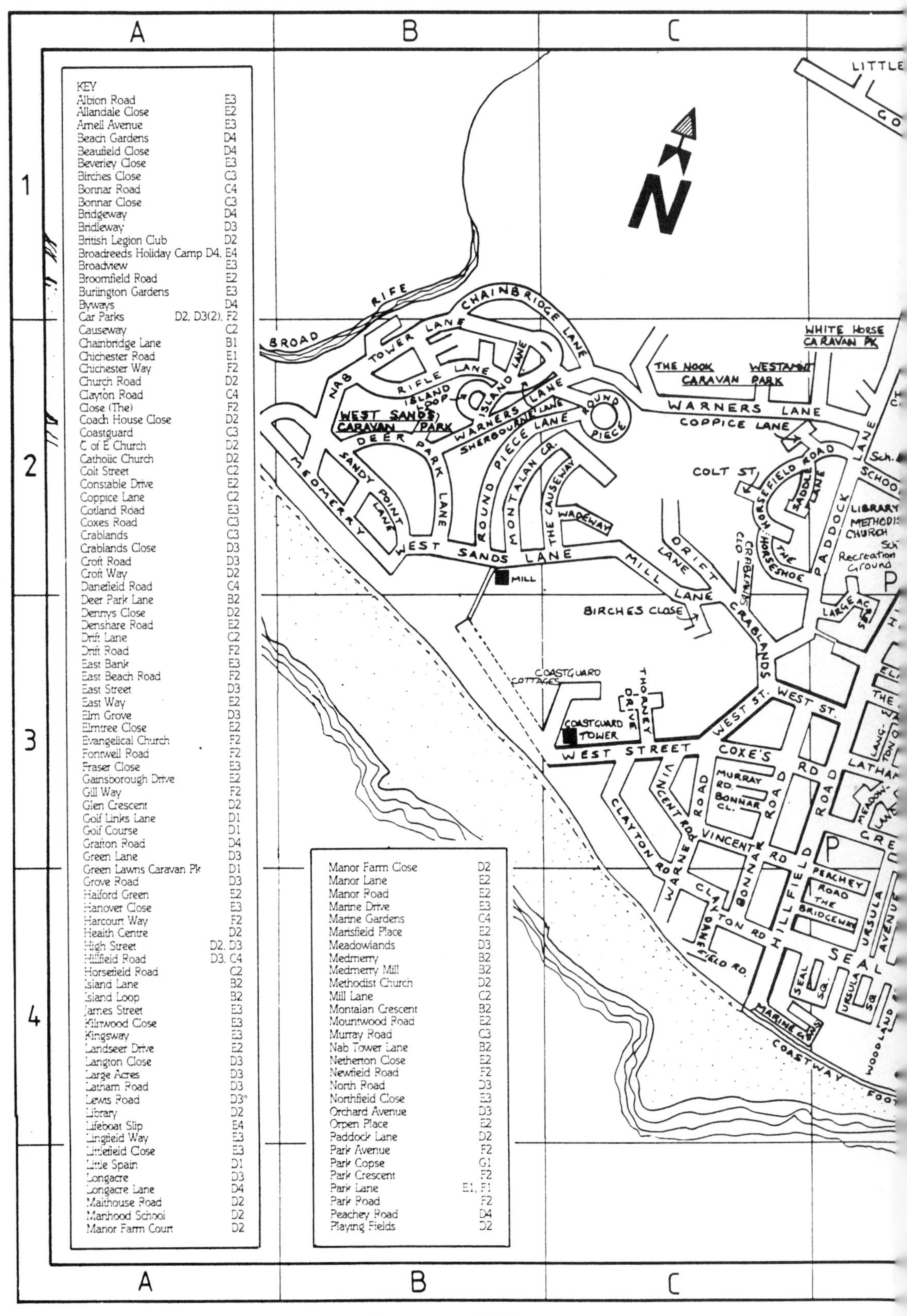

Street map of Selsey.

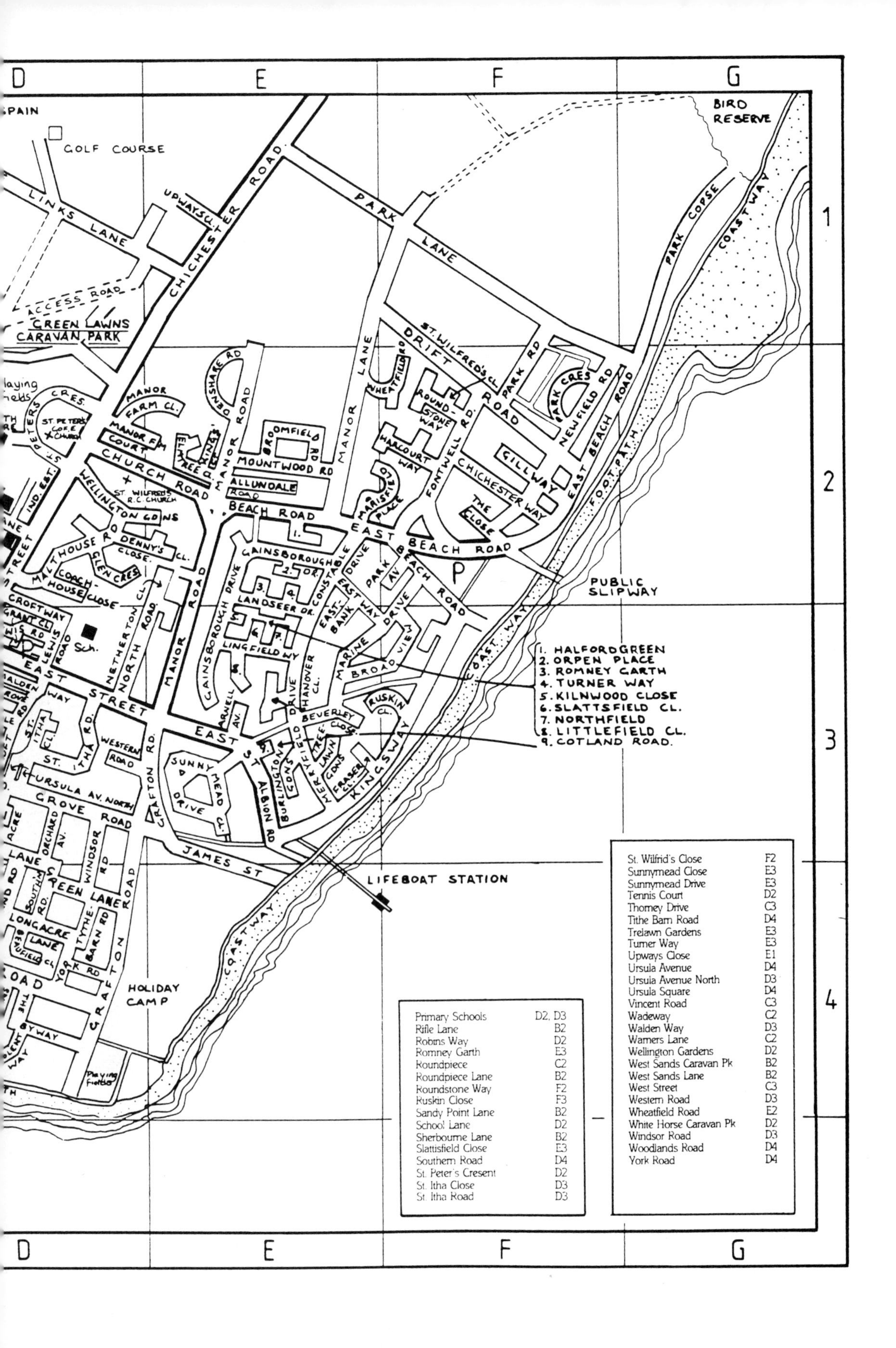
D
E
F
G
1
2
3
4
GOLF COURSE
BIRD RESERVE
LINKS LANE
UPWAYS CL.
CHICHESTER ROAD
PARK LANE
PARK COPSE
COAST WAY
ACCESS ROAD
GREEN LAWNS CARAVAN PARK
ST. PETERS CRES.
ST. PETERS C OF E CHURCH
MANOR FARM CL.
MANOR FM COURT
CHURCH ROAD
DENSHARE RD
MANOR ROAD
BROOMFIELD RD
MOUNTWOOD RD
ALLUNDALE ROAD
ELMTREE CL.
MANOR LANE
WHEATFIELD RD
DRIFT ROAD
ST. WILFRED'S CL.
PARK RD
PARK CRES
NEWFIELD RD
EAST BEACH ROAD
ROUNDSTONE WAY
HARCOURT WAY
FONTWELL RD.
CHICHESTER WAY
GILLWAY
THE CLOSE
MARISFIELD PLACE
FOOTPATH
IND. EST.
ST. WILFRIDS R.C. CHURCH
WELLINGTON GDNS
BEACH ROAD
EAST BEACH ROAD
MALTHOUSE RD
DENNY'S CL.
DENNY'S CLOSE.
GLEN CRES
COACH-HOUSE CLOSE
CROFTWAY
GRANT CL.
LEWIS RD
Sch.
NETHERTON CL.
NORTH ROAD
GAINSBOROUGH DRIVE
CONSTABLE DRIVE
LANDSEER DR.
LINGFIELD WY
EAST WAY
EAST-BANK
PARK AV.
MARINE DRIVE
BROADVIEW
HANOVER CL.
P
PUBLIC SLIPWAY
1. HALFORD GREEN
2. ORPEN PLACE
3. ROMNEY GARTH
4. TURNER WAY
5. KILNWOOD CLOSE
6. SLATTSFIELD CL.
7. NORTHFIELD
8. LITTLEFIELD CL.
9. COTLAND ROAD.
EAST STREET
WALDEN WAY
ST. ITHA CL.
ST. ITHA RD.
WESTERN ROAD
ARNELL AV.
BEVERLEY CLOSE
RUSKIN CL.
KINGSWAY
SUNNYMEAD DRIVE
SUNNYMEAD CL.
ALBION RD
BURLINGTON GDNS
MERRYFIELD
TREELAWN GDNS
FRASER CL.
URSULA AV. NORTH
GROVE ROAD
GRAFTON RD.
ORCHARD AV.
WINDSOR RD
JAMES ST
LIFEBOAT STATION
GREEN LANE
SOUTHERN RD.
TYTHE BARN RD
LONGACRE LANE
YORK RD
GRAFTON ROAD
HOLIDAY CAMP
BYWAY
Playing Fields
Primary Schools D2, D3
Rifle Lane B2
Robins Way D2
Romney Garth E3
Roundpiece C2
Roundpiece Lane B2
Roundstone Way F2
Ruskin Close F3
Sandy Point Lane B2
School Lane D2
Sherbourne Lane B2
Slattisfield Close E3
Southern Road D4
St. Peter's Cresent D2
St. Itha Close D3
St. Itha Road D3
St. Wilfrid's Close F2
Sunnymead Close E3
Sunnymead Drive E3
Tennis Court D2
Thorney Drive C3
Tithe Barn Road D4
Trelawn Gardens E3
Turner Way E3
Upways Close E1
Ursula Avenue D4
Ursula Avenue North D3
Ursula Square D4
Vincent Road C3
Wadeway C2
Walden Way D3
Warners Lane C2
Wellington Gardens D2
West Sands Caravan Pk B2
West Sands Lane B2
West Street C3
Western Road D3
Wheatfield Road E2
White Horse Caravan Pk D2
Windsor Road D3
Woodlands Road D4
York Road D4

People will not look forward to posterity
who never look backward to their ancestors

Edmund Burke

Chapter One

Selsey in its Setting

Selsey has always been a place of unique charm though, sadly, recent development has changed its character, not always for the better. Many older residents will recognise Selsey in this description given by Frank Pairpoint, a visitor from London, in *The Independent Journal* in 1886:

> Here was a fishing village in all its simplicity – a coastguard station with red tiles and white-washed walls, fishermen's huts (all in a rough tumble-down condition, some thatched, others with only a few boards nailed together for a roof); while in front, boats of all sizes and all sorts lay scattered about on the beach, from the sturdy little fishing smack . . . to the rough, weather-beaten old hulk . . . Tubs, full of tar and pitch, wicker baskets, crab and lobster pots, cork, rope, bits of wood, worn-out anchors, and gear of every description, all lying about in endless confusion, helped to make up a most picturesque and interesting sight.

1. Selsey fishermen outside their huts, *c.*1910.

Throughout all periods of history Selsey has frequently been spelt 'Selsea'. This is misleading, though the correct etymology of the name does stress the links between the village and the sea – Selsey is unusual in that it is surrounded by the sea on three sides. One of the earliest explanations of the name is given by Bede in A.D. 683. He spells the word *Seolesige* and interprets it as *quod dicitur Latine insula vituli marini*, that is 'the island of the marine calf', the Latin paraphrase being used to describe the seal.

Selsey, the most southerly parish in Sussex, was an island down to the early years of the 19th century and, today as then, the English Channel surrounds it on two sides, Pagham Harbour lies to the north-east, and the Broad Rife runs from the harbour through the low-lying land to the north of the village, joining the sea on the west at Bracklesham Bay. Bede describes Selsey as 'That place . . . encompassed by the sea on all sides except the west, where is an entrance about the cast of a sling'. The Isle of Selsey, as it is often described in early documents, was connected with the mainland by two fords across Selsey or Pagham Harbour, the Wadeway, and west of it, the Horseway, and by a ferry close to the Wadeway. Until the Ferry Bank was completed in 1809 on the site of the ancient Wadeway, there was a ferryman who held a cottage and land and was paid four bushels of barley a year for his services in 1661. At that time a man and a horse paid twopence and a foot passenger paid a halfpenny to cross to the mainland. The ferry has now been replaced by a bridge carrying the B2145 road from Chichester, which runs south through the hamlet of Norton to Selsey. In about 1930 the road at Ferry was raised and given a concrete surface. Prior to that time there was frequent flooding and bus passengers often took one vehicle from Chichester to Ferry, got off and walked along the embankment, and joined another on the other side! The existence of Ferry Farm House, even today, bears witness to the earlier remoteness of Selsey. Many Selsey residents have developed an 'island mentality' and when they cross 'The Ferry' they think of themselves as back home.

The island probably gained its name from the stranding of a seal there on some memorable occasion, rather than from their common presence in the area, though seals were reported to have been observed in Pagham Harbour opposite Norton in the late 1940s, and in 1951 a baby seal was captured near the lifeboat station and photographed before being taken out to sea by a fisherman. The Chichester Rural District Council coat of arms used to feature a seal prominently. It was once believed that the original place name was 'holy island' (Old English *selig eg*), based on the fact that Christianity in Sussex began with the landing of St Wilfrid in Selsey. This, however, is erroneous, the true Old English name being *seoles eg* or 'seal's island'. By the time of the Domesday survey in 1086 the name had become 'Seleisie'. Later forms are without interest except for the unusual 'Celeseye' in the 1279 Assize Rolls for Sussex and 'Silesia' in the 1338 Calendar of Charter Rolls.

The name Selsey Bill is first seen on Philip Overton's Map of Sussex (1740), and there is no evidence that it is old. The Bill is not particularly beak-like in shape and it may be that the headland is so called in imitation of Portland Bill, where the term is much more appropriate.

Today the village of Selsey is on the edge of the peninsula, but in the distant past it would have occupied the centre. This is due to the gradual washing away of the peninsula by coastal erosion. Selsey Bill is composed of loose sands, sandy clays and a little soft stone, none of which offers much resistance to the constant pounding of the waves. The peninsula is in a particularly exposed position, not protected by the Isle of Wight as is the coast further west.

The erosion of the peninsula has been the subject of comment from the earliest days. For example, in the Nonae Rolls (which dealt with the value of land for tithe purposes), it was claimed in 1340 that in Selsey 'arable land drowned by the sea' accounted for the loss of tithe amounting to £5 6s. 8d. since the valuation of Pope Nicholas in 1272, only 68 years previously. There is clear evidence of erosion from maps of the area. The map reproduced as endpapers was drawn originally in 1672, but the coastlines of 1820 and 1905 were later added.[1] Medmerry Farm stood well inland in 1672, but the 1905 coastline cuts through its rapidly disappearing ruins. It is impossible to state accurately at what rate the erosion of

2. The ruins of Medmerry Farm, *c.*1900.

the peninsula progresses. It has been variously stated as three, six and eight feet each year. By comparing an early map drawn in 1778-83 with the Ordnance Survey Map of the area in 1875 it has been calculated that during that time the distance between Manor Farm, Selsey, and the high-water mark was reduced by 139 yards. This indicates a loss of land at the rate of just over four feet a year. The rate of loss naturally varies at different points on the peninsula. Edward Heron-Allen, for example, estimated that between 1672 and 1911, when he wrote his great work *Selsey Bill: Historic and Prehistoric*, the distance between High House and the high-water mark had been reduced by about 500 yards, giving a general average loss of over six feet a year. Whatever the rate, the loss has been considerable and the coastline continues to change today, though a sea wall was constructed in the 1950s to protect the village. It is now difficult to imagine that a preparatory school, Halton House, stood not far from the site of the present lifeboat station just after the Second World War.

Selsey is situated in the Hundred of Manhood (or Manewode), in the Rape of Chichester. This hundred was a liberty of the Bishop of Chichester, consisting of the land originally given to St Wilfrid by the Saxon King Ceadwalla in A.D. 683. The boundaries of the Hundred of Manhood as described at that time coincided exactly with those recorded in a charter of Henry VIII in 1525. They ran from the entrance of Selsey, or Pagham, Harbour round the coast to 'Hormouth' at the entrance to Chichester Harbour (now West Wittering); then up the estuary to 'Brimesdik' (683) or 'Bremersdytch' (1525), the stream dividing Birdham from Appledram; then eastwards 'to Wayflete, and from thens in circuit into Made-up-lane [now Jury Lane] and so eastward to Dammer-gate; and so along the dytch unto the said Unredisdytch', now Bremere Rife, which runs south into Selsey Harbour. The original Saxon name of the hundred was probably *maene wudu*, meaning 'common wood', though the term may not have referred to the entire peninsula, only the meeting place for the hundred, perhaps in the Earnley/Birdham area.

William the Conqueror divided Sussex into six vertical areas (Chichester, Arundel, Bramber, Lewes, Pevensey and Hastings) called Rapes, each possessing a seaboard, a port, a river, a fortress and a forest. No other county in England was divided in this way. These Rapes may have been ancient Saxon provinces which the Conqueror took over and converted into feudal castleries. The word Rape is derived from the Old English *rap*, meaning first the rope used to fence off a property and later the land itself which had been divided in this way. The parish of Selsey proper was divided into two districts, Norton and Sutton. The former (North Town) survives in Church Norton and the latter (South Town) included the village as we know it today. Selsey commonly occurs under the name Sutton in early deeds and manorial records. Today the Selsey peninsula is noticeably low and treeless. At its highest point it is little more than 30 ft. above sea level and, in spite of the name 'common wood', trees on the peninsula are in very short supply. In earlier times both sides of Pagham Harbour were densely wooded, mainly with fine oaks. Local tradition has it that many trees were cut down to provide timber for the construction of Chichester Cathedral. It is certainly true that woodland was destroyed to get the maximum possible crops from the land during the Napoleonic Wars when there was a nationwide shortage of corn and, more recently, Dutch Elm disease has decimated Selsey's tree population still further, notably in the Crablands area and in Rectory Lane, Norton.

Selsey peninsula has been the site of human habitation since prehistoric times and a great wealth of evidence is available, both in the form of material artefacts and, later, of written records, to chart the history of the village and the men who have lived there.

Chapter Two

In the Beginning

Most of the rocks of which Sussex is composed were laid down under water at an exceedingly remote period when the physical geography and climate of the world were totally different from today's. All the rocks in the Selsey area are part of the Hampshire Basin, and all are young in geological terms. The Selsey peninsula itself is part of the Bracklesham Beds, formed between 50 and 42 million years ago and made up of clays and sands. The Selsey division of these Beds is rich in fossil remains – 400 different species have been found to date. The most common are molluscs, but fragments of shark and ray teeth, and bony fish have been found too, as well as more exotic remains such as crocodiles, turtles, sea snakes, large shells including cowries, corals and the fruit of the Nipa palm which resembles coconuts.[2] The fossils are all of tropical and sub-tropical species because, at the time the Bracklesham Beds were laid down, Britain was in the sub-tropical climate zone. Since then Britain, with the rest of Europe, has drifted north and is now home to creatures requiring much colder conditions. Geological work has been done on the Selsey peninsula in recent years, in particular by Denis Curry and Chris King.

After about 40 million years the Bracklesham Beds were gently folded and the whole area subjected to a long period of erosion. The latest Pleistocene deposits (dating from two million years ago to the present) are found on a fossil platform of marine erosion cut in a warm interglacial period when the sea level was higher than at present. At various times channels filled with a variety of deposits were cut below this level and these have yielded straight-tusked elephant, rhinoceros and mammoth. As the interglacial sea receded, it left a mass of marine shingle which forms the peninsula today. After cold conditions and the cutting of new channels connected with the drowned 'River Solent', rising sea level has led to the deposition of modern alluvium (Pagham Harbour) in the last 10,000 years, which in places is already being removed by modern erosion.

In March 1909 *The West Sussex Gazette* reported that James Lawrence, a Selsey fisherman, had found on the beach, well below the low water mark, a mass of red clay in which was embodied the remains of a mammoth, not fully grown, though 30 ft. in length. Some of the bones weighed several hundredweight. In April 1911 *The Chichester Observer* told of another local fisherman who had brought up a mammoth's tooth weighing nearly 6lbs. while trawling off the Selsey coast. Excavations in the Selsey peat bed in July 1961, led by Dr. Sutcliffe of the British Museum, unearthed the tusk and vertebra of a 100,000-year-old straight-tusked elephant. These are now in the Natural History Museum.

The earliest remains on the peninsula indicating human habitation date from the Palaeolithic period. For example, a Palaeolithic flint knife was found at Medmerry Farm in 1909 in the eroded cliff. In Neolithic times the Selsey area was one of light forest and man probably lived mainly on the Downs. However, there is abundant evidence of Neolithic flint workshops along the coast of the peninsula and single shards of Neolithic B pottery have come to light in Selsey. Neolithic B pottery consisted of round-bottomed bowls with thick rims and deeply concave necks, with exuberant impressed decoration over the outer surface.

Bronze first appeared in Britain around 1800 B.C. and the Bronze Age lasted from then until *c.*500 B.C. Bronze weapons and ornaments are principally found in connection with burial places and most surviving Bronze Age barrows in Sussex are on the chalk downs.

There was some Early Bronze Age occupation along the coastal strip but most of this was destroyed by intensive cultivation and building development. However, it seems that three large barrows must have stood on the Selsey peninsula, between Wittering and Medmerry, for they are referred to in early charters; the name Rumbridge, now lost, is a corruption of Early Middle English *at thrum bergen* which means 'at the three barrows'. An early Bronze Age flat metal axe or celt was found on the coastal plain at Selsey, and at Bracklesham Bay a hoard of flanged axes, dirks and rapiers has been discovered.

In the Late Bronze Age and Early Iron Age gold began to be plentiful – it was probably imported from Ireland. Two gold armlets were picked up on the beach at Selsey in 1925 and 1937. These take the form of an incomplete ring with thickened open ends and are similar to others found elsewhere in the county. They have been dated to between 300 and 200 B.C. Relics of the Iron Age are abundant in the Selsey brick earth. The first Iron Age floor identified at Selsey was discovered on the east coast in 1909 and another Iron Age floor, including fragments of coarse pottery of the period and some worked flints, was found in the cliff opposite Beacon House before it was washed away in the 1920s. A bronze coin from Cnidos, belonging to the second century B.C., has been found at Selsey, indicating foreign trade at that early date. Some historians believe that later in the Iron Age a Belgic city may have been founded on the coastal plain in the Chichester or Selsey district, and that this may have taken the place of the Trundle and Cissbury as a market town. Many remains have been found in the Selsey area: strongly Belgicised pottery, hundreds of early British coins, mostly gold, together with miscellaneous fragments of gold, suggesting the possible site of a mint. In about 1878 some 300 gold coins were picked up which had been washed out upon the clay beds on the shore from Medmerry Farm as far as West Wittering. Other small pieces of gold were found at the same time, including a bar of yellow gold 4½ inches long and weighing 104 grains, and also various pieces of jewellery. Most of these objects were presented to the British Museum. As recently as December 1986 it was reported in *The Chichester Observer* that four gold and 13 silver coins, dating from the Iron Age, had been bought by the Chichester Museum. The coins, valued at between £5,000 and £10,000, had been found in Selsey by a man using his metal detector on a cliff fall.

The use of coins had been adopted by the Belgae who had copied the idea from the Romans, the gold stater of Philip of Macedon, in circulation in Rome in the second century B.C., being the prototype. At one point British coins were only struck in southern and eastern Britain, and it is in Sussex and in Selsey in particular that the greatest number and variety of such coins have been discovered. Some coins were inscribed, and the Roman lettering suggests that they may have been minted subsequent to the arrival of the Roman legions in Britain, though British rulers are known to have employed Roman (or Gaulish) craftsmen and this could account for the 'classical' lettering and design of some of the later British coins. The inscribed coins bear the names of Commius and his three sons, Tincommius, Verica and Eppillus. Commius was in Britain at the time of Caesar's second invasion in 54 B.C. The coins of Tincommius have been found in the greatest quantity on the shores of the Selsey peninsula. By the start of this century 96 coins inscribed with his name had been found in Selsey, 28 of Verica and two of Eppillus. It seems that both Tincommius and Verica ruled the tribe of the Atrebates who occupied West Sussex, Verica probably ousting Tincommius, who is believed to have fled to Rome.

These two brothers presumably ruled their kingdom from a capital city of some kind and the concentration of coins at Selsey suggests it may have been the site chosen for this *oppidum*. Coastal erosion might have prompted the Romans to move the capital to Chichester later, and the Belgic city at Selsey, if it existed, would have been swallowed up by the sea.

A long dyke may once have stretched across the Selsey peninsula from Chichester Harbour, north of Birdham, to the Bremere Rife which flows into Pagham Harbour. Such a dyke (similar to Devil's Ditch which runs from Halnaker to West Stoke, built to protect Chichester) would have served admirably to defend a town in the Selsey area. Evidence for the existence of this earthwork depends on two Saxon charters in which a dyke forms the northern boundary of the Selsey peninsula. In A.D. 683 this earthwork was called Brimesdick, in 957 it appears as Brynes dic, and as late as 1525 it was still a recognisable landmark called Brunesdyke or Bremers dytch. On the Armada map of 1587 the 'Hundred Howse dyke in Manwed' is marked a little distance north-west of Sidlesham church (*see* page 21). Such a dyke would have defended the peninsula from the north, but there is insufficient evidence to prove whether or not the dyke was a Belgic fortification.

After the invasion of Claudius (A.D. 43), native coinage became superfluous. It is likely that when Aulus Plautius invaded, the Britons in Selsey buried their mint stock and jewels, expecting to dig them up again within weeks or months when the Romans left. This time, however, the Romans stayed for 400 years and, only now, over the last century or so, is the sea revealing its secret hoard of our Celtic forebears.

Roman coins almost immediately took the place of British ones. The Roman armies quartered in the neighbourhood would have received their pay in Roman coin, and this quickly passed into general circulation as they bought local goods. Coins have been discovered at Selsey from the time of Hadrian, Marcus Aurelius, Diocletian, Trajan, Vespasian, Nero and Constantine, to name but a few. In 1932 about 1,000 silver Roman coins were found in the garden of 'Halton', Fish Lane, welded by corrosion into a solid mass in a broken crock.[3] They were dated by experts to the third century A.D. There were very few of the poor, almost illegible, coins found in most hoards and this suggests that 'selected' coins may have been buried by a superior officer of the army of occupation, attempting to preserve his treasure from government officials rather than from the barbarian invaders. The garden of 'Halton' may have been on the site of a Roman villa.

Other finds of the Roman period have been made at Selsey. The Ordnance Survey Map of 1899 records the discovery at a point between North Common Farm and Warner's Farm of a Roman urn, though its present whereabouts is unknown. Edward Heron-Allen, the writer, himself discovered large quantities of Roman, Romano-British and Early British pottery in an adjacent gravel pit, including the pieces of a very beautiful and delicate Roman vase, now restored. The find also included fragments of roofing tiles and some highly-glazed fragments, perhaps part of the furnace of the hypocaust of a Roman villa. Fragments of Roman pottery come to light relatively frequently all over Selsey Bill both when the ground is ploughed up and on the surfaces of the alluvium and brick earth exposed along the shore by the erosion of the cliffs. In 1962 a Roman well was found at Selsey on a site known as South Cotland Field, East Street. It was discovered when drains were being dug by a mechanical digger, prior to the building of an estate of bungalows.

Before leaving the earliest inhabitants of the Selsey peninsula, we must consider the Mound in Church Norton, which has been variously described as an Early British earthwork and as a Roman camp. The height of the Mound from the bottom of the trench to the top of the ridge is about 38 ft., and the surrounding ditch varies in width from 25 ft. to 40 ft. across and is about 7 ft. deep. Pagham Harbour was in the past much deeper than it is today and open for shipping. No better place could have been chosen for a fortress or encampment, for the sea came practically to the foot of the Mound, as it does now at high tide. In 1911 the Mound was properly excavated for the first time and it was found to be almost entirely artificial. In the centre is a platform of rough blocks of limestone, held together with cement of the typical Red Roman kind. All round the platform the ground is formed of shingle mixed with lime mortar, indicating that a building of some importance stood on it, possibly a square stone tower. Immediately to the east of the platform must have been a kitchen midden, as the earth was found to be full of bones and teeth of domestic animals and

3. The Mound, Church Norton, looking much less overgrown than it does today. Much more excavation work needs to be done on this earthwork before we can fully understand the part it has played in the history of Selsey.

chickens, fragments of pottery of Roman and medieval date, and quantities of oyster and other shells. Fragments of Roman bricks and roofing tiles were also found. It seems likely, therefore, that a look-out station was erected by the Romans at this place, though insufficient Roman remains have been discovered to prove the existence of a defensive fort before the late Saxon/early Norman structure.

The Romans were not the first to realise the value of the site. The 1911 excavation also revealed fragments of rough pottery of the Iron Age and small ornamentally-worked flints of the late Neolithic or early Iron Age. The Saxons probably built the mound as we see it today: a small Anglo-Saxon belt end made of bronze with beautiful incised ornamentation was discovered, dating from around A.D. 900. It seems fairly certain, then, that the Mound was occupied by the earliest Celtic inhabitants of the peninsula, that the Romans used it as a landing stage and perhaps a look-out station, that the Saxons built a defensive fortification and that throughout medieval times it was occupied by a camp or other settlement. Latest thinking[4] is that the surviving mound is the remains of an 11th-century ringwork which once supported a square tower, the foundations of which were discovered in 1911. The tower may have functioned as a keep, or perhaps a gatehouse since it occurs on one side of the ringwork. The close proximity of the ringwork to St Wilfrid's chapel points towards some relationship between the two. Since the bishopric was not moved from Selsey to Chichester until 1075 (*see* page 15), it is possible that the ringwork was established around the time of the Norman Conquest to protect a church which represented the remains of Wilfrid's seventh-century cathedral. It has always been popularly believed that Wilfrid's cathedral stood at Church Norton: William Rede, Bishop of Chichester, for example, asked in his will for his body to be buried in the chancel of the church, 'formerly the cathedral church of my diocese'. In fact, however, the surviving remains appear to be of the early 13th century although fragments of Anglo-Saxon sculptured stone were built into the present parish church when it was moved to Selsey in the 1860s, and these may have come from Church Norton.

The Mound provides a natural link between the Celts and Romans considered in this chapter and the Anglo-Saxons to be dealt with in the next. It is impossible to conjecture how long the Roman occupation of Selsey lasted but, taking the date of the Roman evacuation of Britain to be A.D. 410, there are over 40 blank years before the invasion of Aella disturbed the post-Roman serenity in the year 457.[5]

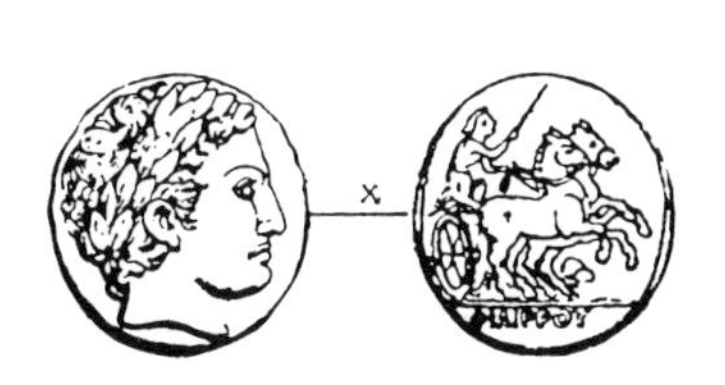

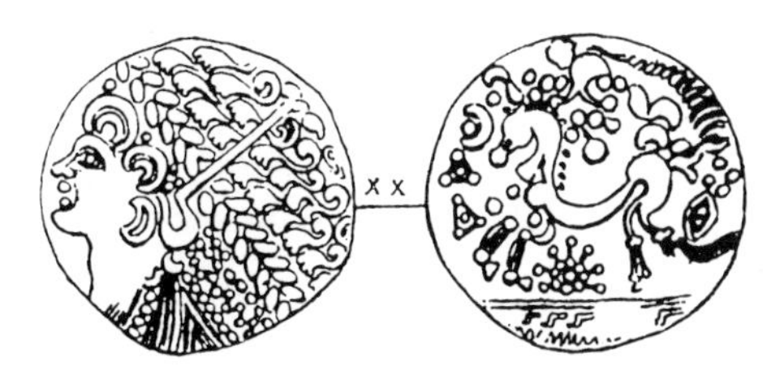

(*Above*) The original gold stater and an example of an early British coin modelled on it and found in Selsey. As time passed, the regal head and the two-horsed chariot became further and further removed from the original design until it was almost unrecognisable.

(*Below*) Drawings of two coins found in Selsey, one with a convex TINC (Tincommius) on a sunk tablet with a prancing horse on the reverse, and the other with a convex VERIC and COMF in two lines with a crescent above and a star below and on the reverse a horse and REX beneath it. The latter was a small, or quarter-sized, coin of Verica.

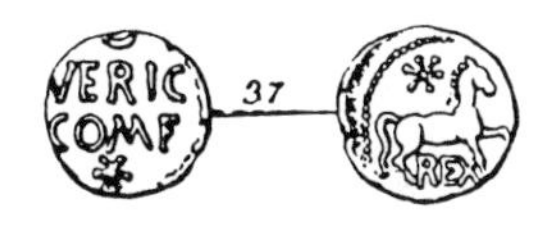

Chapter Three

The Coming of Christianity: 457-1075

In A.D. 457 Aella, a Saxon warrior, with his three sons Cymen, Wlencing and Cissa, is thought to have landed his forces at Cymenes-ora (the shore of Cymen), near the southern tip of the Selsey peninsula, though a landing in East Sussex cannot be ruled out. The name is still traceable in Keynor Farm, which stretches down to the shores of Pagham Harbour, and in Keynor Lane which runs from Sidlesham to Highleigh. It is probable that at first he was content to establish a bridgehead in Selsey, then virtually an island, while receiving reinforcements from the Continent. It may well be that the Mound at Church Norton was part of Aella's first defence work. In the 1930s evidence was discovered of Saxon settlement in the area west of the remains of Medmerry Farm, brought to light by erosion of the cliffs. Pottery, animal bones, charcoal, oyster and winkle shells, loom weights and parts of querns were all found and dated to the Saxon period. It is possible that during the fifth century Owers Bank formed the coastline and so this settlement would have been well inland. Aella was followed as ruler by his son Cissa. After his death the kingdom of the South Saxons, or Sussex, relapsed into a very barbarous condition, cut off from neighbouring kingdoms and the influences of Christianity by the marshes, the sea and the forest (Andredesweald). Sussex was the last Anglo-Saxon kingdom to forsake the old pagan gods. In 607 Sussex was absorbed into the kingdom of the West Saxons, or Wessex, but in 661 became independent again under Ethelwald, King of Sussex, who may perhaps have lived at Kingsham (the royal estate), south of Chichester.

In A.D. 681 Wilfrid (634-709), Bishop of York, who had been expelled from Northumbria because of his antagonism to the reigning monarch, arrived in Sussex, doubtless at the invitation of Ethelwald, who gave him hospitality and granted him land in the Isle of Selsey. Wilfrid was probably the first Englishman of culture and learning who had pierced the mighty forest of Anderida, 120 miles long and 30 miles wide, extending from Kent to Hampshire. His arrival was destined to spread Christianity and civilisation within Sussex, though he cannot be said to have introduced Christianity to the kingdom, since Ethelwald himself had already embraced the new faith in one god some time earlier.

Bede tells us that:

> for taking his way into the province of the South Saxons, which extends from Kent . . . as far as the West Saxons, and contains land of 7,000 families, who at that time were still pagans, he administered to them the word of faith, and the baptism of salvation . . . Bishop Wilfrid, by preaching to them, not only delivered them from the misery of perpetual damnation, but also from an inexhaustible calamity of temporal death, for no rain had fallen in that province in three years before his arrival, whereupon a dreadful famine ensued, which cruelly destroyed the people . . . But on the very day on which the nation received the baptism of faith, there fell a soft but plentiful rain; and the verdure being restored to the fields, the season was pleasant and fruitful . . . the bishop, when he came into the province, and found so great misery from famine, taught them to get their food by fishing; for their sea and rivers abounded in fish, but the people had no skill to take them, except eels alone . . . At this time, king Ethelwalch gave to the most reverend prelate, Wilfrid, land of eighty-seven families, to maintain his company, who were in banishment, which place is called Selesea, that is, the island of the sea-calf . . . Bishop Wilfrid, having this place given him, founded therein a monastery, which his successors possess to this day.

Wilfrid was granted 87 hides: a hide was the unit of land measurement, which in the seventh century meant land able to support one family. A charter dated A.D. 683 names some of the land given: 'Seolesige, Medeminige, Wihittringes, Iccannore, Bridham, Sidelesham', that is Selsey, Medmerry, Wittering, Itchenor, Birdham and Sidlesham. Wilfrid, therefore, was granted a sizeable block of land around Selsey itself, though the charter also mentions more distant villages scattered around Sussex, for example Aldingbourne, Mundham and Amberley.

Wilfrid was a man of outstanding character – Bede informs us that he was handsome, charming and graceful, pious and learned. As well as teaching the people of Selsey to fish (a skill he acquired in Fresia), he manumitted 250 slaves, both men and women, during his time in Sussex. Among his first acts were the erection of a cathedral, and a monastery in which his followers could live. Wilfrid was a great builder: he created cathedrals of beauty in both Ripon and York, using stone masons and glaziers brought from France. He was also a great advocate of the monastic life, being the first to introduce the Benedictine order in this country and founding almost 80 monasteries during his lifetime. He dedicated the cathedral at Selsey to St Peter,[6] doubtless remembering his own cathedral church of St Peter at York. Little remains of this cathedral at Selsey today and no records or drawings exist to show us what it looked like. The structure known to St Wilfrid may well have been of a very primitive wattle and daub type. Perhaps the most important vestiges are two remarkable sculptures preserved in Chichester Cathedral. They were discovered behind some stall work in the choir in 1829, probably hidden there to save them from destruction during the siege of Chichester in 1643. Carved out of Caen stone, the sculptures, which are primitive but remarkably vivid, represent the raising of Lazarus and the meeting of Jesus with Mary and Martha. According to F. M. Bond, 'The figures are the tall, emaciated, but dignified figures of Archaic Byzantine art, their stature carefully proportioned to their importance'.[7] These sculptures have long been reputed to be Saxon work, but some historians, including Dr. Kendrick who wrote on the subject in *Late Saxon and Viking Art*, feel that the style of carving points to a date not earlier than A.D. 1100.

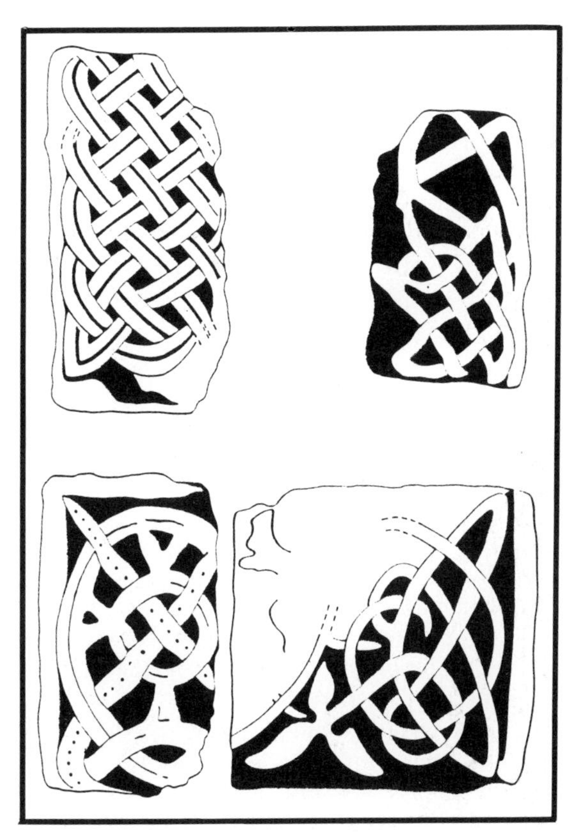

4. Carved Saxon stones, part of an early palm cross probably erected by St Wilfrid and now incorporated into the war memorial in Selsey churchyard.

Another possible relic from Wilfrid's cathedral is the font, still in the parish church in Selsey today, which is of typical Saxon four-square design. This font was mentioned in the Archdeacon's visitation in 1636 when it was stated that 'this ffont will not hold water and hath not a fitting cover'. The font is made of Purbeck marble and stands on a central shaft surrounded by four small shafts. As indicated by the visitation report, the font was badly damaged but has been restored in recent times by the letting in of blocks of matching marble. It may have come from St Wilfrid's cathedral, though some historians have dated it to the 12th century.

Stones have also been discovered, elaborately carved with typical Saxon interlacing and scroll work. Eminent architects and archaeologists who have examined them are convinced of their Anglo-Saxon origin and feel they probably came from the cathedral church. They may well have formed part of the upright shaft of a very early cross. A palm cross at Selsey is frequently mentioned in ancient documents, especially early wills. In 1545, for example, Geoffrey Thomson, a Rector of Selsey, directed by his will that his body be buried 'before the Palm Cross in Selsey Churchyard'. A cross still stands in the churchyard of Bewcastle in Cumberland, which is known to have been erected by Wilfrid in A.D. 670. The decorations and carvings are in every respect identical with the Selsey fragments, two of which were found built into the wall of a summerhouse at Grange Farm, Church Norton, in 1911, and two inside the porch of Selsey church which may have come from Norton. These fragments have now been incorporated into the war memorial set up in Selsey churchyard in 1920.

Finally, a Selsey fisherman trawling off the coast of the peninsula brought up in 1909 a primitively but accurately sculptured foot in Caen stone, Saxon in style and workmanship. These waters, east of Selsey, are called the Park. It is recorded that there was a deer park in that vicinity in Tudor times. Most of this is now under the sea, though a little has survived. Some of the deer park has been incorporated into the gardens of the bungalows north of 'Noah's Ark' in Copse Road, but there are still a few acres near the inland salt lakes called the Severalls. William Camden, the famous antiquary and historian (1551-1623), claimed that in his time the ruins of the Saxon cathedral were 'at low water evidente and plain to be seen'. While most people, from Camden down to Edward Heron-Allen and the majority of Selsey residents today, believe St Wilfrid's cathedral to have been washed away by the sea, there are a few dissenters from this traditional view, including the historian Dr. John Fines. The anomaly of the Saxon palm cross alone provides grounds for doubting this charming story. The cross would certainly have stood within the precincts of the cathedral and probably fairly near to the building itself. Yet as late as the 1540s, not long before Camden wrote about the submerged cathedral, a Rector of Selsey was asking to be buried next to it. If the cross was not washed away by the sea, perhaps the cathedral was not either. The greatest part of the cathedral would have been constructed of wood and once the See was moved to Chichester in 1075 official funds would no longer have been forthcoming for its maintenance and the parishioners of Selsey would not have been able or even willing to pay from their own pockets for repair work on the disused building. The explanation for the disappearance of the cathedral, sited as it was in Norton where there does not seem to have been as much coastal erosion as there was further south, may lie simply with the ravages of time and weather and the plundering of what stone there was for other uses.

The community which came to Selsey with Wilfrid was doubtless a mixed body of clergy, secular and regular, and laymen in the capacity of servants. They were probably organised according to the Benedictine rule at first but, as time went on, the community consisted wholly of secular canons. Of the original monastic building it is doubtful if a single stone remains, but a building still standing today as Norton Priory, which until 1903 was the Rectory House of Selsey, is of great antiquity. Records show that there was a Rectory on the monastic site in the early 13th century, and Saxon herring-bone work, identical with the seventh- and eighth-century work in St Wilfrid's crypt in York Minster, can be seen in the footings of its walls. Norton Priory as it now stands, however, was largely built in the 15th century. It is possible that the ruins of the Roman villa or military station on the site of the nearby Mound may have afforded building materials to Wilfrid when he founded at

Selsey his Episcopal College of Secular Canons, which survived at least until the Norman Conquest in 1066.

Many great blocks of stone, dug out of the surrounding marshes and ditches and preserved in the rock garden at Norton Priory, show traces of having once formed part of a church – there are round sections of pillars, fragments of cornice stones and dressed stones of all dimensions. In one part of the garden is a square stone, its sides carefully cross-hatched, containing a deep basin, evidently a holy water stoup. Early this century the owner of Norton Priory presented a small, perfectly preserved holy water stoup to the Duke of Norfolk which is now in the chapel at Arundel Castle. Both were brought to the Priory by fishermen who had dredged them in their trawls out at sea, where the site of the old cathedral is popularly believed to be. It is possible that the Priory occupies the actual site of St Wilfrid's monastery.

In 681 St Wilfrid established his Bishopric at Selsey. During his time in the area, Ceadwalla came from Wessex and attacked Kent, Sussex and the Isle of Wight. Ethelwald fell in battle and soon Sussex was completely under the sway of Ceadwalla. He was converted to Christianity by Wilfrid and confirmed the lands already granted to the See of Selsey. Theodore Bernardi, a Flemish artist, painted in 1519 a huge picture which represents the interview between Ceadwalla and St Wilfrid. The painting now hangs in Chichester Cathedral. In the corner may be seen Selsey church and the Priory, with the entrance to Pagham Harbour beyond, as they appeared in the early 16th century. The conversation between the two men appears in Latin on scrolls. Wilfrid says to the king, *Da servis Dei locum habitationis propter Deum* (Give to the servants of God a dwelling place for God's sake), and the king replies, *Fiat sicut petitur* (Let it be as thou desirest).[8]

Ecfrith, the Northumbrian king who had driven Wilfrid into exile, was killed in battle in 685 and soon after this Wilfrid was restored to his See of York. He died in 709 and his body was first interred at Ripon but afterwards translated to Canterbury. He had no further personal connection with Selsey after his return to York. In the Cathedral Statutes of Chichester are found the following regulations concerning the observance of St Wilfrid's Day (12 October): 'That the feast of St. Wilfrid be celebrated in the Church of Chichester all the more devoutly because he had converted the heathen of the parts [round] Chichester to Christ.'

From the coming of Wilfrid in 681 till the removal of the See to Chichester in 1075, the history of Selsey is the history of its bishops and their cathedral church. There were 24 Bishops of Selsey in all. The spelling of the bishops' names varies considerably in different chronicles, as does the year in which they were consecrated.

Very little is known about most of these bishops except that they appended their signatures in their episcopal capacity to numerous extant charters whose subject matter frequently has little to do with Selsey. Their portraits in the north transept of Chichester Cathedral, painted by Bernardi in 1519, are of course purely fanciful – all their faces look alike and they are wearing 16th-century costumes!

After the departure of Wilfrid, the kingdom of Sussex was an appendage of Wessex. In temporal matters Sussex was subject to the West Saxon kings and in ecclesiastical matters it was subject to the Bishops of Winchester. However, in A.D. 705, King Ine, successor to Ceadwalla, resolved to divide the diocese of Winchester, by now too unwieldy due to the extension of the kingdom of Wessex. A new See was established at Sherborne and four years later the See of Selsey was revived. Wilfrid's clergy had remained at Selsey after his departure. Edbright was the president of the brotherhood and in 709 he was consecrated Bishop of Selsey, after a vacancy of 24 years.

More evidence is available for a few of Selsey's bishops. In 780 Gysseur or Gislhere succeeded to the bishopric. This was the year of one of the most important documents in the Anglo-Saxon history of Selsey – the Charter of Oslac. This charter was rediscovered in

Year of Consecration (approx.)	**Name of Bishop**
681	Wilfrid
709	Edbright
714	Ella
733	Segelyn
761	Aelbright
765	Bosy
780	Gyssuer/Gislhere
785	Thoha
789	Pethun/Wethun
811	Ethelwiff
824	Ceadret
860	Godard/Gutheard
909	Bernegus/Beornege
931	Wulfhun
944	Elured/Alfred
963	Athelyn
980	Algar/Aethelgar
989	Ordebright
1009	Aylmar
1032	Aglebright
1039	Grymketill
1047	Heda/Hetta
1058	Aethelric
1070	Stigand

1891 by Rev. John Cavis-Brown of Selsey in a concealed and long-forgotten drawer in Chichester Cathedral. Oslac was Duke of the South Saxons in A.D. 780. The text of his charter is in Latin and is contained on a single sheet of vellum or parchment. Below is a translation:

> Our Lord Jesus Christ reigning and ruling for ever! I Oslac, Duke of the South Saxons, freely grant a certain part of the land for the benefit of my soul to the venerable Church of S. Paul the Apostle, that is (it is known) by two names, Earnaleach (or) Tieloes-or, with all thereto appertaining things, fields, woods. In the year of the Incarnation of the Lord DCCLXXX, this was done in the place which is called Siolesaei.

Oslac and Gislhere both signed the document and on the reverse it has been endorsed by Offa, King of Mercia. The Church of St Paul the Apostle evidently refers to the cathedral of Selsey. There is some doubt as to the original dedication of the cathedral. It may have been to the Virgin Mary, to St Peter or St Paul, or perhaps there was a joint dedication to the two saints which would explain the wording in the text. Earnaleach is the modern Earnley. Oslac's Charter is the only place where the name Selsey appears as Siolesaei.

The next bishop of note was Gutheard or Godard, head of the See at the time of the Danish invasion. The absence of Selsey charters at this time may be an indication of the suspension of business of a peaceful character. Between 838 and 909 the only extant signature of a bishop of Selsey is by Bishop Gutheard. The See may possibly have lain vacant during part of these troubled times. In the final struggle with the Danes at the end of Alfred's reign, a Danish army harried the South Saxons near Chichester in 895 but were put to flight and many of their ships were taken, according to W. R. W. Stephens.[9] Selsey was probably protected from the Danes by the sea in front and the marshy, wooded land behind. Also the religious community was poor compared with the monasteries of regulars, so the invaders would not have been drawn to it for plunder.

Bernegus or Beornege was bishop of Selsey at the time of the revival of learning and ecclesiastical prosperity under Alfred and his grandsons Athelstan, Edmund and Edgar. Athelstan may have had a residence at Chichester. In 930 he granted to Beornege the manor of Medemeninga (Medmerry) 'with the wood and fields adjacent thereto called Earneleia' (Earnley). It seems likely that the old cathedral of Selsey was greatly improved or perhaps rebuilt during the episcopacy of Beornege.

Only one bishop of Selsey was ever raised to the exalted heights of Canterbury. That was Aethelgar or Algar who became bishop of Selsey in 980, having been trained by St Dunstan at Glastonbury. He administered Selsey for eight years, before being translated to Canterbury.

Ordebright and Aylmar were bishops of Selsey during the reign of Ethelred the Unready when the Danes crossed year after year from their favourite winter quarters on the Isle of Wight. They made for the harbours at Chichester and Bosham, and appear to have left Selsey unmolested. Aglebright came to the See when Canute (1017-35) had restored peace to the kingdom. These must have been prosperous times for Selsey as Godwin, the mighty Earl of Wessex and friend of the king, had a residence at Bosham. Also Aglebright was an intimate friend of the Archbishop of Canterbury of the time, and was in fact buried beside him in Canterbury Cathedral.

Aethelric, a monk from Canterbury, is considered by some historians to have been the last bishop of Selsey, because his successor, Stigand, is always recorded as the first bishop of Chichester. When William the Conqueror landed he found Aethelric established at Selsey,

> then far advanced in years, and of the highest reputation for his knowledge of the Saxon laws. Upon this account that venerable prelate was not displaced, but was greatly esteemed by the new monarch and consulted by him upon all questions of the ancient national jurisprudence.[10]

But in 1070 Aethelric was deposed by William and confined at Marlborough. After the Conquest, Selsey probably became a port of communication between England and Normandy, both by reason of its geographical proximity with France and because of its natural advantages as a haven.

In 1070 the King gave to his chaplain, Stigand, 'the bishopric of the South Saxons' – he was in reality the last bishop of Selsey because the See remained there for the first five years of his episcopate. The religious establishment at Selsey was probably not wholly relinquished until the buildings at Chichester were ready, and Chichester Cathedral was not finally complete until 1145. It was general Norman policy to move Sees from rural areas to towns, as agreed at the Council of London in 1075; at the same time as Selsey was moved, the bishopric of Sherborne was transferred to Salisbury and that of Lichfield to Chester. It may also be that the Normans felt Selsey was too close to the sea for comfort. St Richard became the patron saint of the new cathedral and now only the little chapel at Church Norton remains as a reminder of St Wilfrid and the importance of Selsey in the religious history of Sussex. The cathedral and monastic buildings lie under the sea, forgotten by all but a few.

As Stephens wrote, 'It requires an effort of mind to grasp the idea that there were twenty-four Bishops of the South Saxons who had their cathedral church on the storm-beaten shores of Selsey for three hundred and fifty years – as long a period as that which separates the reign of Queen Victoria from that of Henry VIII.'[11]

Bishop Stigand died in 1087, and from that time till the appropriation of the episcopal estates by Queen Elizabeth in 1561, the history of Selsey is dominated by its lords of the manor.

Chapter Four

The Episcopal Manor of Selsey: 1075-1561

The trees of the Andredesweald which had saved Sussex and Selsey from occupation by the Danes were no defence against the determination of a warrior like William of Normandy. He came with a task force of 90 ships and 6,000 soldiers, and landed unopposed at Pevensey Bay in September 1066. It was difficult for the English King Harold to raise recruits from the men of Sussex for his army to save England from foreign domination. Most of those who were not fishermen were farmers and it was harvest time. For the men of Selsey, like those throughout the county, 1066 was just another year and Harold's call to arms just another interference with the essential business of reaping. After the Battle of Hastings a large number of Harold's army, mostly Sussex men, lay dead. The survivors of that day paid for their loyalty to Harold by having their houses confiscated and a feudal system imposed on them by which they held their land in return for military and other services to their lord. But the men of Kent, who had refused to come to Harold's aid, were allowed by the Norman occupiers to retain their own legal system and were under no obligation to do military service. William Horsfield, the great Sussex historian, wrote in 1835: 'The cultivators of the soil of Sussex in those days were rendered in fact the absolute property of the Lord of the Manor who sold, exchanged and punished them at his will or pleasure'.

During the winter of 1085 William ordered the Domesday survey to be made to ensure that he was getting all he should from the annual tax on every hide of arable land – to the fury of the men of Sussex this was raised from 2s. to 6s. in 1086. This survey was made at a critical time in the history of Selsey, at the moment when the episcopal See was removed to Chichester. In Domesday Book Selsey is classified in the Rape of Chichester and in Somerley Hundred. This later became the Hundred of Manhood and comprised the estates of the Bishop of Chichester at Selsey, Sidlesham and Wittering.

The Domesday entry for Selsey states *Ipse episcopus tenet Seleisie in domino*, that is, the Bishop himself holds Selsey in lordship. The Bishop of Chichester would have held some of the land in Selsey in demesne for his own use and would have let some out to tenants, such as William and Geoffrey. Both in 1066 and in 1086 there were 10 hides of land in Selsey,[12] sufficient to employ seven plough teams, each consisting of eight oxen. The villagers and cottagers, in return for land sublet to them by the bishop, would have to perform work on his demesne farm. They were theoretically chattels of the manor, though they appear to have acquired certain privileges. The slaves, however, were wholly under the sway of the Bishop. The entire manor at the time of Edward the Confessor was valued at £12 (the Norman *libra* or pound was worth 240 pennyweights of sterling silver, or 20 shillings); its value later dropped to £10, but by the time of Domesday it had been restored to £12. By omitting all reference to swine in Selsey, the survey reveals that there were no woods on the episcopal domains at that time, for woods were always valued according to the number of pigs to which they gave pasturage.

The concept of the manor and the manor house seems to have originated with the Norman Conquest. By that time the manor was regarded as a taxable unit. Though Selsey manor had always had a separate existence of its own, for some fiscal purposes it formed part of the larger manor or hundred of the Manhood, whose hundred or manor house was just north of Sidlesham church. The earliest court rolls of the manor of Selsey date from 1455, though they are by no means all extant after that time. There are also some 'Minister's

Ipſe eps ten SELEISIE . in dñio . T.R.E. 7 m̄ ſe defd p . x . hid.
Tra . ē . VII . car . In dñio ſunt . II . car . 7 XVI . uitti cū XI . bord . hñt
. V . car . Ibi . II . ſerui . 7 VI . hagæ in Ciceſtre de . XXXVIII . denar.
De iſto M̄ ten Goisfrid . I . hid . 7 Witts dimid hid . 7 dim uirga.
7 hñt . I . car 7 dimid . cū uno bord.
Tot M̄ T.R.E. ualeb XII . lib . 7 poſt: X . lib . Modo dñiū epi: XII . lib.
Hōum ej: XL . ſol.

SELSEY, in lordship. Before 1066 and now it answered for 10 hides. Land for 7 ploughs. In lordship 2 ploughs.
16 villagers with 11 smallholders have 5 ploughs.
2 slaves; 6 sites in Chichester at 38d.
Geoffrey holds 1 hide of this manor; William ½ hide and ½ virgate. They have 1½ ploughs, with 1 smallholder.
Value of the whole manor before 1066 £12; later £10; now, the Bishop's lordship £12; his men's 40s.

5. The entry relating to Selsey in Domesday Book.

Accounts', giving details of receipts and expenditure by the bishop's stewards. There are many such accounts in the Public Record Office, dating from 1301 to 1478, and much early domestic history of Selsey can be gleaned from these. There were 42 episcopal lords of Selsey Manor before its severance from the See of Chichester early in Queen Elizabeth's reign. Stigand, who became bishop in 1070, was the first and William Barlow, consecrated in 1559, was the last. Some deserve special mention for the light they throw on the story of Selsey.

Seffrid I became bishop and lord of the manor in 1125. To him and his successors Henry I granted the privilege of a fair to be held in Selsey every year for three days, beginning on the eve of St Lawrence the Martyr (9, 10 and 11 August). All merchants and traders attending Selsey fair were, by royal order, to be free from all hindrance in going or returning. This was later confirmed in charters by Henry IV and Henry VI. The privilege was a significant one because, other than at this fair, Selsey residents would have had to buy provisions at Chichester market or from the occasional itinerant pedlar. The fair had a chequered existence as a pleasure fair in Victorian times, but by the 1930s Selsey was being visited by travelling shows and fairs and there were many complaints about the noise, particularly from the steam organs.

Some of the lords of the manor played an important part on the national stage. Bishop Hilary in the 12th century, for example, was chaplain to Matilda, wife of King Stephen, and was also a prominent supporter of the king in his quarrels with Thomas à Becket, his neighbour at Pagham. Similarly, Ranulph was one of the signatories of Magna Carta. All we know of him in connection with Selsey, however, is that on his manor there he owned 20 oxen, 10 cows, one bull and 500 sheep.

Much more light is thrown on the manor of Selsey in the time of Ralph Neville, bishop from 1224, through the letters of his steward, Simon de Seinliz, which were discovered in 1841. The news he gives of the Selsey peninsula is varied and unusual. In one letter he says, 'I think you should know that the Vicar of Mundham keeps two wives', and in another, 'I am working marl at Selsey, because the best marl is found there'. He is probably referring to Sidlesham where there is an outcrop of marl, a limy clay often used as manure. In the calendar of Charter Rolls there are four charters of Henry III, dated 1227, 1228, 1231 and 1233, granting to Bishop Ralph Neville and his successors 'all his liberties in warrens and chaces, woods and plains, in Selsey, Witteringes, Sydlesham and all Manwode', as in the Charter of Ceadwalla.

Richard of Wych was the only lord of the manor of Selsey to become a saint. He was canonised in 1262 by Pope Urban IV. He is associated with various miracles, some of which occurred on the Selsey peninsula. According to Mark Antony Lower in *The Worthies of Sussex*, 'Richard being once at his manor of Cakeham in West Wittering, in a season of scarcity, so great a multitude of people flocked thither that he had not bread enough to feed them all. His servitors were therefore fain to cook beans for the rest, the Saint by his blessing causing the beans to suffice the need of three times as many as they would ordinarily have fed.' On another occasion he is said to have cured Richard, his bailiff at Cakeham, of gout.

Apart from the saintly Richard of Wych, bishops of this period were more lords of the manor than prelates. From the episcopacy of Gilbert de Sancto Leofardo we have the earliest known Minister's Account, that of John de Campenden, 'of expenses incurred at Selsey, collecting and gathering the fruits of the Prebend of Seleseye in the 29th year of King Edward [1301]'. This gives an interesting glimpse into the domestic history of the manor. Under expenses headed 'Autumn' are: 2 quarters of corn for the Lord's stock (13s. 4d.), beer (29s.), cider (20d.), flesh of ox, hog and swine (18s. 5d.), herrings (22d.), barley bought (2s. 3d.), 2 bushels of powdered salt (6d.), soap and candles (8d.) and firewood (22d.). Other expenses outlined include, 'In shoeing horses for autumn period, 8d.', 'In silver given to the household for their gloves 2s.' and 'For rebuilding a wall in a small kitchen 2s. 6d.'

Other medieval bishops were more statesmen than prelates. John of Langton and Robert de Stratford were both Chancellors of England in the 14th century. Robert was plagued by poachers on his lands at Selsey, deer, hares, rabbits, partridges and pheasants all being taken. Smuggling was another problem at this time. While William Rede was lord of the manor several men of Selsey were appointed to search 'in the port of Wydering, and parts adjacent, for persons, except well-known merchants, going out of the realm with gold, silver, jewels or letters of exchange'. To William Rede is ascribed the rebuilding of the old church at Norton between 1369 and 1385. By his will he asked for his body to be buried by the high altar of his manorial church there, but this was disregarded by his executors and he was interred in Chichester Cathedral.

Adam Moleyns, who became lord of the manor of Selsey in 1446, had earlier been Secretary to the Privy Council and Keeper of the Privy Seal. As a favourite of Henry VI he was granted important privileges, including the exemption of all coastland belonging to the Bishop and Church of Chichester from the power and jurisdiction of the Court of Admiralty. He was empowered by another charter of Henry VI to 'impark' 1,000 acres of land in West Wittering and Cakeham, and to wall in and protect his manor houses at Selsey, Sidlesham, Wittering and Cakeham. During his lordship, a manorial court ordered the village stocks and ducking stool to be repaired, under penalty of a fine of 20 shillings.

Moleyns was murdered in 1450 in a boat at Portsmouth, by seamen said by some to have been hired to commit the crime by the future King Richard III.

Nothing has been said yet about the parochial clergy of Selsey. No records exist between 1075 and 1324 when entries relating to Selsey begin in the Registers of the Bishopric of Chichester. However, there is a document in the Patent Rolls, dated 30 October 1450, recording the grant of:

> Pardon to William Pendere, Rector of the Church of Selsey, County Sussex, of the King's suit against him for having, with others, on Wednesday, after St Bartholomew [24 August], 28 Henry VI, at Brembre, Stenynge, Vitelworth [Bramber, Steyning and Fittleworth], with other traitors, rebels, and enemies of the King, there and elsewhere in Sussex, plotted the destruction of the King and realm, and agreed that they and other traitors, lollards, and hereticks, should take upon them the power and rule of the realm, and destroy the lords spiritual and temporal . . .

This is the only recorded part played by Selsey in Jack Cade's insurrection, surprising perhaps, because the widespread suffering caused by the poll tax levied on every person over the age of 15 had been aggravated by the levying of a tax on all fish landed, in order to pay for improved defence of the Sussex coast against attacks by the French. This must have hit Selsey's fishermen severely.

Robert Sherburne was bishop from 1508 to 1536. He set the finances of the parish of Selsey in order, actually lived in the manor house there and probably restored and improved it. In April 1535 he granted the lease of the park at Selsey to John and Agatha Lews (Lewes), whose monument stands in the old chancel at Church Norton to this day. The lease granted the park for 80 years at the rent of £4 and the demesnes at £13 6s. 8d. It was agreed that Lewes should leave sufficient grazing for 70 or 80 deer.

There were many changes of bishops in the mid-16th century because of the cataclysmic events of the Reformation and shifts of royal ecclesiastical policy. During the episcopacy of Richard Sampson, who became bishop in 1536 and spent some time in the Tower for preaching a sermon advocating Popish doctrines, testimony is given to the excellence of Selsey's cockles. In March 1538 William, Earl of Southampton, wrote to Thomas Cromwell: 'I have sent you by bearer certain Celsey cockles. No doubt you are daily furnished with them by my Lord of Chichester, who is lord of the soil where they be had'.

William Barlow, consecrated in 1559, was the last episcopal lord of the manor of Selsey. In 1561 Elizabeth I passed an Act which severed the manor of Selsey from the See of Chichester. The Queen appropriated eight manors at this time, including both Selsey and Sidlesham, paying no regard to the protests of her bishops. At this time 'the Manor of Celsey is of the clear yearly value of £53 4s. 10½d.'. In this way Selsey passed from episcopal hands, after being held by 24 bishops of Selsey and 42 of Chichester, into the hands of lay proprietors.

Chapter Five

The Manor of Selsey, 1561-1900

When Queen Elizabeth annexed the Manor of Selsey, the tenant was John Lewes. He died in 1568 leaving the 'fearme and parke at Selsey' to his second wife, Mary. She died in 1578 and the manor passed to Thomas Lewknor, M.P. for Midhurst on two occasions, who was married to Lewes's daughter, Bridget. It then passed to their son, Sir Lewis Lewknor, a document in the Patent Rolls of 1597 granting to Lewis and his son for their lives the lease of 'the Grange, of Selsey Isle, Sussex, at a rent of £20 6s. 8d.'. This lease was given up by Sir Lewis to the Crown in 1612 in return for the payment of £100. In the first year of the reign of James I (1603) the Manor of Selsey, among others, had been granted as a jointure to his consort, Anne of Denmark. She then granted to Sir William Fagg:

> All the Grange, of the Island of Selsey, in the County of Sussex . . . with all the demesne lands, meadows, pastures, feedings, warrens of conies . . . and half part of all wreck of the sea which should happen within the precincts of the said Isle of Selsey . . . And all houses, edifices, buildings, barns, stables, dove-houses, gardens, orchards . . . heath commons, waters, fishing, and fishing-places . . . for eighty years, if the said William Fagg, the father, John Fagg and William Fagg, his sons, and every or any of them should so long live, under certain rents therein mentioned, to be paid to the said Queen for life, and after to the King and his successors.

The rent was fixed at £56 2s. 0½d., a large increase on the £4 paid by Lewes.

Much was happening on the Isle of Selsey while these changes in ownership of the lease of the manor were taking place. In the 1580s Sussex was preparing itself for possible invasion by the Spanish, who were building up their fleet of ships. The earliest existing map of Selsey Bill (*see* illustration 6) seems to be that appended to a survey made in 1587 with a view to improving the defence of the Sussex coast against the Spanish Armada. It reported:

> All the coaste alongste from Cakam Stone,[13] and likewise the Isle of Selsey, and so unto Pagham Beacons, for the moste parte good landinge, and therefore not sufficiently garded, with the partes in the speciall places at A, B, C, but have nede of Trenches or Flanckers artificially founde to be reared in moste conveniente partes for small shott.

The places marked A, B and C as needing improved defences were Cakeham, East Norton (south of Church Norton and probably near the present East Beach) and Pagham Harbour respectively.

The Selsey peninsula has undergone very great changes since this survey was made. The beacons marked on the map have naturally disappeared – they would have been piles of brushwood or furze erected in elevated positions which, when lit, would communicate news of the impending invasion far and wide. The Selsey beacon was positioned some hundreds of yards in front of what is now the holiday camp, and an old house there, which disappeared more than 60 years ago, was known as Beacon House. This house was in danger of being washed away by the sea, due to coastal erosion, but Mr. Ralph Selsby undertook its demolition before that could happen and much of the material was used in building and extending other houses in the village. The dove-houses described as 'a mark at sea' at both Bracklesham and the point of Selsey Bill have long since been engulfed by the sea.[14] The Chichester road is clearly marked as 'The waye from Selsey ferrie to Chichester', and the position of the ferry is pin-pointed. This map is the only one to mark the precise position of the Hundred House of the Hundred of Manhood (here called 'Manwed'), so it is a very valuable document. It is thought that the Mound at Norton was made higher on the seaward

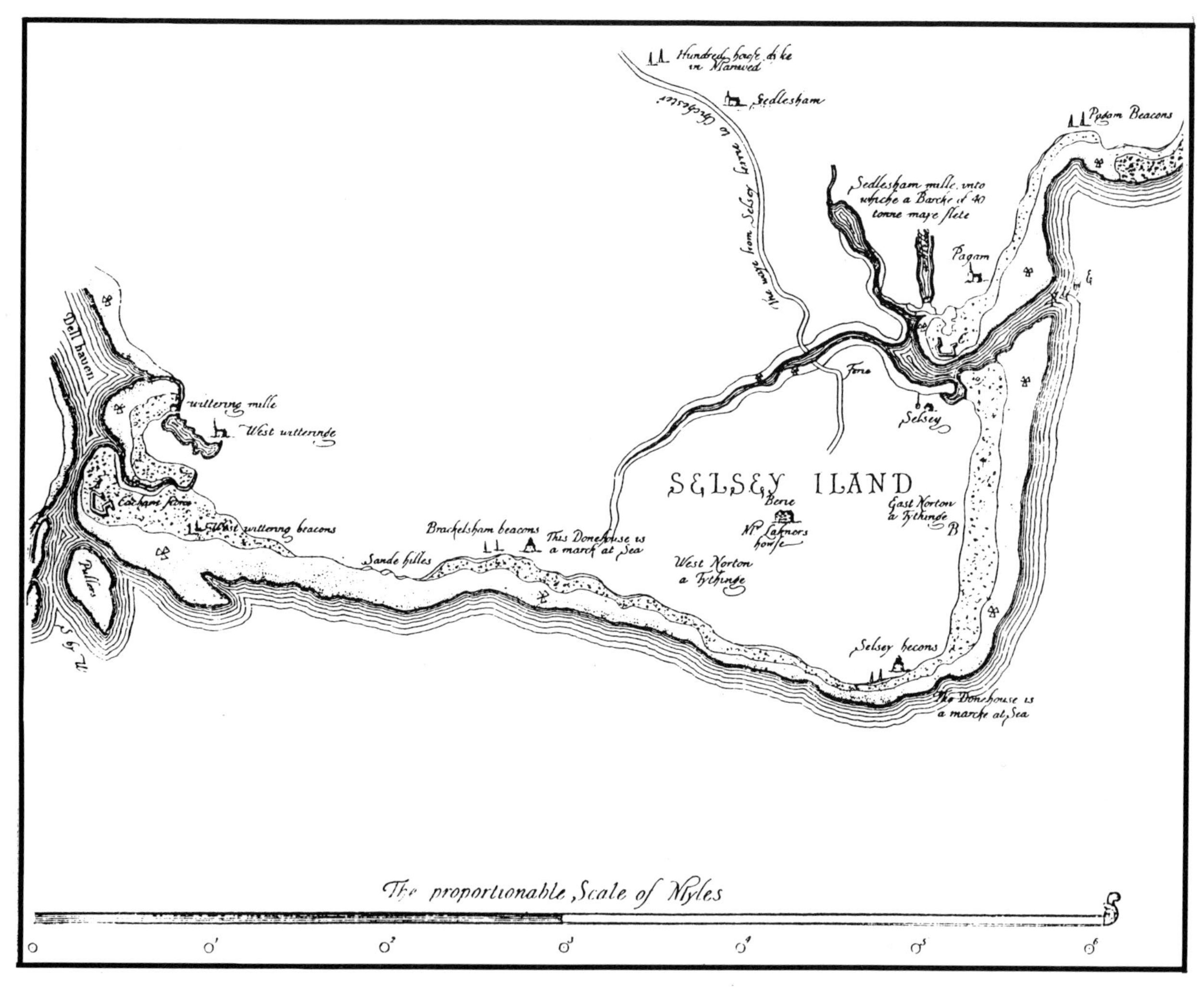

6. Map of the Selsey peninsula from a survey made in 1587 at the time of the Armada invasion threat. Note the position of Selsey, on the edge of Pagham Harbour, the area known as Church Norton today.

side during this time of danger though the evidence for this is slight, resting mainly on a conversation between Mr. A. Rusbridge (author of *Legend of the Mound at Selsey Old Church*) and some workmen in 1911 about a cannon ball dug out of the ditch there.

We have no means of knowing whether the projected defences were carried out or the Selsey beacon lit, but the precautions were in fact unnecessary because in July 1588, when the Spanish fleet arrived off the Isle of Wight with the intention of attacking Portsmouth, the wind shifted to the south-west and blew on shore. Thomas Fenner, captain of the *Nonpareil* and one of four West Wittering brothers to serve under Drake, devised a scheme to drive the Armada on to the Owers Rocks. However, the Spanish Admiral recognised the

7. Beacon House when it was a boarding house with A. Woodland as proprietor. The weekly rates were between £1 15s. and £2 'according to season and rooms chosen'. This card is postmarked 1905.

8. Beacon House in about 1927. Much of the building material had been salvaged for re-use before the sea could claim it.

danger, decided not to resist the English fleet but sailed up the Channel and left Selsey alone, anchoring off Calais. There was a nationwide celebration of the 400th anniversary of the sighting of the Spanish Armada on 19 July 1988, and a series of beacons were lit along the south coast. Twenty-five were lit in Sussex, including one at Selsey. A metal brazier was erected in East Beach car park.

Some information can be gleaned about the lives of ordinary Selsey folk in the 16th and 17th centuries. A document of 1565 tells us that Selsey had 11 fishing boats at that time, and the case of Elizabeth Egley, wife of John Egley, churchwarden at the parish church, gives us a fascinating glimpse of contemporary social traditions. On 15 April 1606 at the Court of the Hundred of Manhood, 'the jurors present that Elizabeth Egley, of Selsey, is a common scold, and therefore the Headborough of Selsey is commanded to cause her to be sett in the ducking-stool, and to be ducked three times over head and ears in the sea'. This drastic measure does not appear to have had much effect for in October of the same year Elizabeth was disciplined in the same way again. The ducking stool was not the only form of punishment on the peninsula. In March 1614 the hundred court recorded that the whipping post of Sidlesham had been uprooted; it was ordered to be re-erected before Easter, under a penalty of 3s. 4d.

We can also gain some idea of the population of Selsey in the Tudor and Stuart period. The Court Rolls of the Manor of Selsey in August 1609 list 99 tenants in all; a similar list in 1555 had named 49 tenants, and back in Bishop Sherburne's time (1522) there had been only 25.

In Charles I's reign, by a warrant under the Privy Seal dated 1628, the King assigned the Manor of Selsey to the City of London which was to have the rents from the land in return for money advanced to the King. The Crown, however, reserved rights over forests, parks, and ecclesiastical benefices. After this there were various changes in the ownership of the lease of the manor, but finally in 1635 it was granted to Sir William Morley I, a Royalist who forfeited the estate during the Civil War and only regained it after paying a fine of £1,000. During the war, the men of East Sussex mainly sided with Parliament which held all the Cinque Ports, but in West Sussex many of the great families were strongly Royalist. Charles Thomas-Stanford, in *Sussex in the Great Civil War and the Interregnum, 1642-1660*, writes: 'Of the gentry, especially in West Sussex, numerous leading families, some of them Catholic, took the King's part, among them may be named . . . the Morley's of Halnaker and the Lewknors', both important families in the history of Selsey. The village appears to have escaped the horrors attendant upon Waller's sack of Chichester and the destruction of its cathedral and churches. But it had a narrow escape. In one of Charles I's letters, written at Naseby in March 1645, he mentions the ease with which the foreign troops on which he relied might 'land at divers fit and safe places of landing upon the west coasts, besides the ports under my obedience, as Selsey near Chichester'.

The majority of the people of Selsey were not Catholic in sympathy, however, for in February 1641/2 the 'inhabitants of the Parish of Selsie, from the age of 18 years and uppwards' signed a protestation against popery and popish innovations and in support of the rites and ceremonies of the Church of England. There were 112 signatories as well as the vicar, churchwardens and overseer. Later, in 1676, a religious census was undertaken for the Bishop of London and Archbishop of Canterbury, from which it appears that in Selsey there were 266 Anglicans, three Protestant Nonconformists and no Papists.

Many of the early rectors of Selsey were pluralists, responsible for many parishes, often far distant from one another, so that it was necessary for the spiritual welfare of the parishioners for a priest to be appointed actually to live among the people of the parish. The first such vicar of Selsey was John Hungerford, appointed in 1513 on terms of continuous residence in the parish. Vicars were always poorly paid and in the 17th century a large number of livings had to be augmented. Between 1656 and 1658 £20 was granted to the minister of Selsey each year on top of his normal stipend. It seems that some Selsey vicars may not have deserved a high salary. Henry Kent, an incumbent in the 17th century, managed to alienate most of his parishioners, according to petitions found in the Sessions Rolls. He told people who would not play cards in the alehouses with him that they would be damned, and preached in 'such kinde of doctrine and in such outrageous words and rayling manner spoken that it rather affrighteth and feareth most of his hearers than edyfieth them'.

The villagers of Selsey had to pay tithes to the Rector. These were a form of taxation consisting of one-tenth of a man's property or produce, but payable only on things that yielded an annual increase by the act of God. There are records of an Exchequer case in 1674 between William Goble, agent for the Rector of Selsey, and Thomas Pearley, a local tenant. In 1665 Goble visited Pearley in his barn at Selsey and demanded a tithe of lambs. There were, apparently, 40 lambs of sufficient age to tithe and Pearley drew out nine for himself and told Goble he might take the tenth lamb for his tithe. Goble refused, alleging that this went against the custom in the village that the owner should first choose two lambs and the Rector take the third, then the owner choose seven and the Rector the next, then the owner take nine more and the Rector the tenth, until all the lambs were fully tithed. Lambs were then worth 3s. each. There were similar unwritten rules concerning other animals. If, for example, a farmer had only one calf and killed it for his family's use, the Rector would be given the best shoulder. If the farmer weaned the calf, the Rector would have only one halfpenny, but if the calf was sold, the Rector would have one-tenth of the value of the sale. At Easter every householder paid the Rector four eggs or a penny in lieu. Long before the Tithe Commutation Acts of 1836-60, tithes were no longer paid in kind in this feudal fashion. For example, in 1832 the total tithe to be paid to the Rev. Barré Phipps (the first man to hold the title of both rector and vicar of Selsey) was £759 13s. 6d. After legal commutation a few years later, the amount agreed on between the Rector and the Selsey tithe payers was £907 12s. 9d. At that time the total area of the parish was 3,494 acres.

The ownership of the lease of the manor changed frequently due to marriages, mortgages, sales and deaths. For a long time in the 18th and 19th centuries it was in the hands of the Peachey family, commemorated in Peachey Road. Sir James Peachey was lord of the manor from 1765. He was Master of the Robes to George IV and was created Baron of Selsey in 1794. It was written at this time, 'The whole is valued at about £1,700 a year, the land being cultivated with wheat . . . The present Lord of the Manor is Sir James Peachey, Bart. and the Manor Farm, which is near a mile south of the church [still at Norton at that time], is worth about £400 a year'.[15] The manor left the Peachey family in 1871. The last customary Court of the Manor is believed to have been held in December 1909.

Selsey is naturally protected from seaward invasion by a chain of reefs around the coastline from Chichester, round the Bill and east as far as Littlehampton. Strong and uncertain tidal currents also help by rendering navigation very dangerous. The first seamarks used in navigation were prominent objects ashore such as church towers and high land. Cakeham tower and Medmerry barn (washed away around 1890) were marked on early maps as fulfilling this function. Medmerry was often used in conjunction with the spire of Chichester Cathedral to enable sailors to get their bearings and avoid the treacherous Mixon Rocks. However, in 1793 the first artificial beacon in Sussex was put up on these rocks south of Selsey Bill because of the dangers of French invasion during the Napoleonic Wars. This beacon was replaced by a new one in 1856.

There is a stretch of shore on the east side of Selsey Bill still known as 'the Barracks'. The name commemorates the Selsey Infantry Barracks, the building of which was begun in October 1803 and completed in March 1804 as a result of the Bonaparte scare. It provided accommodation for 16 officers and 330 men in huts constructed of English oak and wood from Memel in Prussia, as well as hospital beds for 50 patients and stabling for 20 horses. The Barracks were built on the site of a battery of three 36-pounders established in the 1790s to protect the stretch of sea known as the Park after the alliance of French and Spanish sea power. The battery was not elaborate, possibly no more than a high earthen rampart fronting the sea to give the guns height as they were fired over the water. Also in the 1790s a signal station was established in Selsey, east of the sea end of Highfield Road. This would have been a wooden hut in the charge of a naval lieutenant, assisted by a midshipman and two seamen. Outside would have been a tall mast for raising signal flags, by which the Selsey station could pass information about enemy movements to the next station around the coast. During the Napoleonic Wars Sussex mustered almost 6,000 volunteers, of whom 114 artillerymen were contributed by Selsey under the command of Captain Thomas Souter.

William Shepherd, churchwarden, died in 1927 at a great age. He had been a living repository of ancient Selsey lore and, according to newspaper reports after his death, used to recount tales of men who had been 'drawn' for the militia in 1806. Those who did not want to serve used to meet in a public house and bid for substitutes in the persons of men who had not been drawn and who put themselves 'up for auction' to serve. Large sums of money often changed hands. The parish registers give the names of men of various regiments buried in Selsey in 1807 and 1808 and *The Hampshire Telegraph and Sussex Chronicle* reported in October 1808: 'A party of the 89th and 72nd Regiments, about sixty, were landed on Saturday, at the Depot at Selsey, part of whom came from the Cape of Good Hope, afflicted with the ophthalmia, and others are daily expected from the Mediterranean. There are now upwards of 400 men afflicted with the dreadful disorder in the Barracks of Bognor, Aldwick and Selsey.' The Barracks were demolished in 1812 and by 1820 the land on which they stood had gone under the sea.

Soon after this, by an Act of Parliament of 1819 entitled 'An Act for Inclosing Lands in the Parish of Selsey', the common fields were enclosed and fixed areas allotted to the various tenants. At the same time two new public highways were built: a continuation of West Street from High House down to the seashore, and a continuation of the High Street from the corner of West Street down to the sea where the *Marine Hotel* stood, until then only a cart track. The latter was officially called Hillfield Road because it ran through a common field of that name but, right up until the mid-1930s, it was commonly referred to as 'New Road'. The road now named East Street used to be called Cotland Lane because it ran through Cotland Field – this name may well refer to the 'cottars' who each had a plot of five or six acres, or one cotland, for their maintenance instead of wages. It seems a pity that this historic name has been superseded. As late as 1899 *Kelly's Directory* describes Selsey as a village consisting of three streets – East Street, West Street and High Street – and even in the 1950s most roads other than these were private and maintained by local residents.

The preamble to the Selsey Enclosure Act stated that there were open common fields known as North, Hill, Mill and Deane Fields, containing 460 acres, and pasture land called the Mill Greens and North Field Greens, containing 134 acres, upon which occupiers had rights of common pasture, and other open common fields known as Upper and Lower Cotland Field, containing 75 acres. The tenants of these fields had stated that 'their lands were greatly intermixed and dispersed, and were consequently inconvenient and incapable of considerable improvements'. Enclosure and the ending of the ancient but ineffective strip system of farming must, therefore, have been welcomed by the Selsey tenants. No objection was made to the allocation of land made by the commissioners appointed by the Act, nor to the proposed scheme of roads. In 1835 T. W. Horsfield in his *The History, Antiquities and*

Topography of the County of Sussex stated that the parish of Selsey contained 2,880 acres, chiefly arable land, and produced 'average crops of wheat, barley, oats, peas and a few beans'. Selsey's soil was said to be a strong loam on a sandy subsoil and the land on the peninsula was at that time rented out at £1,800 p.a., individual farms varying from £50 to £400.

By the 19th century regular population censuses were being made which are a great help to the local historian in his researches. In 1801 the population of Selsey was 564, by 1851 it had risen to 934 and by 1901 to 1,258, comprising 312 families living in 300 inhabited houses. As late as 1931 Selsey had only 2,513 permanent residents, though the 1981 census revealed 7,745 inhabitants. Flesh can be added to these bare statistical bones by looking at other records. Accounts of churchwardens, elected each year, reveal the names of families whose descendants still live in Selsey today. Names which occur frequently throughout the 17th, 18th and 19th centuries are Woodland, Woodman, Sheppard (or Shepherd), Sherrington, Penfold, Stubington, Copis (or Coplis), Clayton, Mould (or Mold), Tadd, Jinman (or Ginman) and Arnell. The first recorded Woodland was John, taxed 12d. for a subsidy levied on the Hundred of Manhood in 1295. The Woodlands, Arnells and Claytons have been so prominent in the history of Selsey that each of the families has a road named in its honour – Woodland Road, running parallel to Hillfield Road down towards the point of the Bill; Arnell Avenue, off Albion Road; and Clayton Road between West Street and Warner Road. The naming of roads after local families has continued up to the present day. A bungalow development was named Grant Close in 1982 after the family which has had such close connections with the lifeboat service in the village over the years. Mike Grant is coxswain at the moment, and his father held the post for a number of years, too. Census records from 1851 onwards give the place of birth of residents: the vast majority, with the exception of coastguard officials and some schoolteachers, were born in Selsey itself or settlements nearby such as Sidlesham, Pagham, the Witterings, Birdham or Mundham. It is also interesting to note that throughout the 19th century by far the greatest proportion of Selsey men were classified as either fishermen or agricultural labourers.

The tomb of John and Agatha Lewes in St Wilfrid's chapel, Church Norton

Chapter Six

The Village at Worship

The Parish Church of St Peter

The date of the original foundation of Selsey parish church, prior to its removal from Church Norton to its present site in 1866, is unknown. It is possible that it was built from materials remaining from the early cathedral and that it was rebuilt by Bishop William Rede in the 14th century – this would account for his desire to be buried there. Dallaway wrote of the church in 1815, 'It is large, and consists of a nave and two aisles, ceiled with oak, and divided by arches, common at the close of the 14th century'. In fact four of the arches, still in the building today, are of late 12th-century work. Other features on which Dallaway remarked are the Purbeck marble font, referred to on page 11, and four coffin-shaped slabs of marble, decorated with crosses, which are now tucked away on the floor against the walls of the old chancel at Norton, oak pews fastened over them. These slabs, three of Purbeck marble and one of Caen stone, formerly marked the tombs of rectors of the parish and date from the 13th century. There is also a canopied tomb of John Lewes and his wife (*see* page 19) kneeling at a desk, he in armour and with his hair bobbed, she in a gown, mantle and bonnet. The inscription behind the figures reads: 'Here lyeth Jhon Lews and Agas his wife, which Agas dep'tyd this AD 1537'.

9. Selsey church at Norton: an engraving from the *Gentleman's Magazine*, 1798.

Reminders of the power of the sea are never far away anywhere in Selsey. A stone in the shadow of the ancient chancel covers the grave of two young men drowned in Trafalgar year in an attempt to save others from the same fate. The inscription by William Hayley is now illegible but once read in part:

Around this grave with veneration tread,
For youth and valour graced these honoured dead;
Grac'd and yet failed their youthful lives to save
From the dark rage of winter's ruthless wave.

The old church was extraordinarily rich in shrines or chapels, sometimes referred to as 'lights'. John Rede, in his will of 1517, bequeathed 4d. for every light in the church and Richard Walter, in 1531, bequeathed 2d. to each of St James's, St Mary's, St Katherine's, St Margaret's and St Nicholas's lights. At the time of the suppression of the monasteries in Henry VIII's reign, these shrines were destroyed and much of the stone and marble used for secular building.

Some interesting details have been unearthed about the condition of the parish and the church when it was situated at Norton from records of visitations by bishops. In 1578 Selsey folk reported, 'Wee had no sermon theis twoo yeres. The walls and fence about the churchyard are in grete decay, and so is our church steeple'. By 1724 there were 'about a hundred families', and no Catholics or Dissenters in the parish. 'During summer half-year there is preaching twice a Sunday, and catechizing; the other half of the year there is only morning service and once preaching . . . Sacrament three times a year, at Easter, Whitsuntide, and Christmas. Number of communicants twenty-five or thirty'. Sometimes more general details about the village are revealed in these reports, such as in 1772 when the bishop recorded that there were in Selsey no hospital, almshouses or free school, and no doctor or midwife.

At this time there was a ruined tower at the west end of the church, visible in old photographs of the building at Norton. This represents the original vestry which fell into

10. Selsey church before its removal from Church Norton in 1866, showing the ruined vestry at the west end. This photograph was taken between 1856 and 1864 by James G. Russell of Chichester – the restored cresting tiles and flagstaff on the tower enable it to be dated this precisely.

EDDI, priest of St. Wilfrid
In his chapel at Manhood End,
Ordered a midnight service
For such as cared to attend.

But the Saxons were keeping Christmas,
And the night was stormy as well.
Nobody came to service,
Though Eddi rang the bell.

"Wicked weather for walking",
Said Eddi of Manhood End.
"But I must go on with the service
For such as care to attend."

The altar-lamps were lighted,—
An old marsh-donkey came,
Bold as a guest invited,
And stared at the guttering flame.

The storm beat on at the windows,
The water splashed on the floor,
And a wet, yoke-weary bullock
Pushed in through the open door.

"How do I know what is greatest,
How do I know what is least?
That is My Father's business,"
Said Eddi, Wilfrid's priest.

"But—three are gathered together—
Listen to me and attend.
I bring good news my brethren!"
Said Eddi of Manhood End.

And he told the Ox of a Manger
And a Stall in Bethlehem,
And he spoke to the Ass of a Rider,
That rode to Jerusalem.

They steamed and dripped in the chancel,
They listened and never stirred,
While, just as though they were Bishops,
Eddi preached them The Word,

Till the gale blew off on the marshes
And the windows showed the day,
And the Ox and the Ass together
Wheeled and clattered away.

And when the Saxons mocked him,
Said Eddi of Manhood End,
"I dare not shut His chapel
On such as care to attend."

11. 'Eddi's Service' by Rudyard Kipling. Eddi was St Wilfrid's chaplain and biographer, Eddius Stephanus.

ruin before 1805. When the church was removed in 1866, the ruins were cleared away and a new vestry added on the north side of the chancel.

The social life of Selsey does not ever appear to have been concentrated around the old church at Norton. This area was the residence of the landowners, while the bulk of parishioners lived in Sutton, Selsey village. The major part of the congregation, therefore, had to walk two miles to church and in 1864 serious agitation for the removal of the building to its present site began.

In July 1864 a Parish Vestry meeting authorised the raising of £600 towards the expenses of removal, on the security of the Church Rate, the remainder of the cost, £3,000, being defrayed by the Hon. Mrs. Vernon-Harcourt, Lady of the Manor, who lived at West Dean Park and was heiress to the last Lord Selsey.[16] She also presented the community with the new site at the top of the village. No new materials had to be bought, for the church at Norton was to be rebuilt in Selsey and the stone from the ruined tower there was available for any additional work required. Some antiquaries expressed fears that a fine old Early English church would disappear but the Rector, Rev. Henry Foster, reassured them in his long and meticulous account of the removal of the church in *The Standard* in September 1864, which is virtually an 'apologia':

> We are going, not merely to pull Selsey Church down, but to build Selsey Church up again . . . stone for stone, as it now stands. The site of the building will be changed, not the building itself. It will be some two miles from its present site, and no longer two miles away from my parishioners, but among them – Selsey Church restored . . . The existing chancel of Selsey Church will remain . . . It will form a chapel for burials.

He mentions several specific features of the church, explaining for example that the font will be restored to make it as much as possible as it would have been in the 11th century.

There would be some changes – he mentions the 'frightfull bell-cot at the west end, which mars the general appearance of the Church. In the restored Church this will give place to a stately single spire'.

His chief justification for the removal of the church is for the convenience of his parishioners. He states that when he first came to Selsey in 1863 the population of the parish was 900, but the average church congregation was scarcely 100. He felt this was largely because, for a good 750 of the population, the church was between two and three miles from their homes. The expense on the parish would be too great if a new church was to be built and both that and the old church at Norton had to be maintained, so the obvious solution was to move the old church to a more convenient site. Rudyard Kipling's poem, 'Eddi's Service', describing a midnight mass which only animals managed to attend, may be a rather fanciful indication of the remoteness of the church at Norton even in the seventh century. (Eddi was St Wilfrid's chaplain, Eddius Stephanus.)

Demolition of the church began in 1864 and stones were transported on farm carts to the new site. The re-erected church with its new chancel was finally consecrated in April 1866. There were some changes, such as the addition of a vestry, the building of the spire and new bells, cast at the Whitechapel foundry. The stone fabric of the nave was transported, together with the magnificent oak roof. The church today is a most attractive one, with

12. St Peter's church in 1930, showing the spire and war memorial. The view was then more open than it is today because St Peter's Crescent had not been built to the south of the church.

13. St Wilfrid's chapel, Norton, in 1935: the chancel left behind when the parish church was moved to Selsey in 1866.

14. Aerial view of St Peter's church in 1928 showing the new rectory built in 1903. The church hall now stands on the site of this rectory. Note the manor house at the top of the photograph, today surrounded by other buildings.

many fascinating features. There is a magnificent lectern, believed to be pre-Reformation in date, which came from Chichester Cathedral. It represents an eagle perched on a globe and is said to symbolise the Word of God winging its way across the continents of the world. Norton's early Norman font was transferred to Selsey as was the church plate, including an Elizabethan communion cup engraved with the words 'For Selsey Pari'. The windows are more modern, but splendid none the less. The east window, for example, created by Messrs. Kempe & Co., portrays the risen Lord and in the background the Sea of Galilee with its fishing smacks, most appropriate for Selsey. This window was dedicated in 1917 to the memory of two Selsey men killed in the Great War.

Under ecclesiastical law a church could be moved but not its chancel, so the old chancel was left at Norton and was described in 1904 as 'derelict, unhappy, a home for bats and owls'. However, in 1905, when the church of St Martin in Chichester was pulled down, the late Rector gave the communion table and hangings, as well as 12 fine oak pews, to Norton. The roof was repaired, the walls painted and the paths regravelled. Also the old churchyard was extended and the building, renamed St Wilfrid's chapel in 1917, is still used to this day. Communion services are held there about six times a year by the Rector of St Peter's, including one on St Wilfrid's Day (12 October). Selsey Catholics also use the building on occasions, particularly for a Requiem Mass on All Souls' Day. A joint Anglican and Catholic pilgrimage was made to the chapel in 1981 to celebrate the 1300th anniversary of St Wilfrid's landing. Burials take place at Norton rather than on the Selsey site, though nowadays more and more funeral services are held at St Peter's where the mourners can have the benefit of heating and organ music. The chapel was included in a list of buildings of special architectural or historic interest in 1958.

At first the rectory continued to be at Norton. *Kelly's Directory* for 1899 mentions this rectory, with its 51 acres of glebe land and the vicar's net income of £530. In 1902, on the appointment of a new rector, Rev. John Cavis-Brown, the old Rectory at Norton was sold and a new Rectory at Selsey was completed in November 1903 on two acres of land adjoining the church, bought for £214. It was designed to accommodate his 10 children and domestic staff and cost almost £4,000 to build, but the size of the building became an embarrassment to his successors. It has now been demolished and was replaced by a new house in St Peter's Crescent in 1974. The name of the old Rectory was changed to Norton Priory (*see* chapter three).

Rev. Cavis-Brown died in 1909, following a stroke, and was succeeded by Rev. C. W. G. Wilson. During his incumbency the Bishop of Chichester, Dr. Ridgeway, visited Selsey, on 7 June 1912, to dedicate a new organ presented to the parish by Edward Heron-Allen as a memorial to his father, and a new organ chamber provided by the parishioners. This replaced an earlier organ, paid for in 1867 by the Hon. Mrs. Harcourt. At the close of the dedication, a recital was given. The new organ was a fine two-manual instrument with oak casework, the chamber itself having been built by a local man, Mr. T. E. Bonnar. It is still used today. In May 1915 *The Chichester Observer* reported that the Rev. Wilson had been appointed Vicar of Cuckfield. The report claimed: 'By all classes, including summer visitors, he is regarded with the utmost esteem, and by the fishing fraternity of Selsey he has been looked upon as a real friend'. A silver loving cup and the sum of £70 was presented to Rev. Wilson as a parting gift at a ceremony at the cinema hall. An illuminated address contained the subscribers' names, and these included a large number of nonconformists as well as church people which attests to the poularity of the man throughout the village. He was well known for his work as Chairman of the Managers of both the Church of England and Council schools and in support of the Selsey branch of the National Lifeboat Institute. He was followed by the Rev. K. H. MacDermott, Vicar of Bosham, who was Rector of Selsey from 1915 to 1925. He was a musician of considerable talent and played an organ voluntary before the start of each Sunday service.

The removal of the church to the main centre of the population seems to have had the desired effect of encouraging more parishioners to attend services. In March 1897 the Bishop of Chichester attended St Peter's to confirm 31 candidates from the parish, 12 boys and 19 girls. This speaks volumes about the change in the population structure of the village during the last century as well as about the decline in general church attendance. In 1915 there were 28 baptisms, 13 marriages and 19 burials in Selsey parish church, indicating a flourishing community. In fact, the church seems to have been a model of its kind, if a report in *The West Sussex Gazette* of February 1916 is to be believed. This stated:

> There is no trouble to get people to the Church at Selsey. The difficulty is to find seats for them when they are there, and this at all times of the year. Regular members are being urged to come a little early to relieve the churchwardens of difficulty. Not only is the attendance at the church good, but the singing is hearty, the responses are well made, and the attention of the congregation is earnest and devout.

In June 1921 *The Chichester Observer* recorded that a fund was being raised towards the cost of erecting a church hall on a site in West Street, generously given by Miss H. W. Clayton, an old Selsey resident. It was to be used for social functions, lectures and meetings and would supply a long-felt need in the village. In fact, a church hall was finally built in the High Street, the original site having been sold. The foundation stone was laid in October 1923 and Miss Clayton opened the building in May 1924. It was a simple building, well lit inside and capable of seating 200 people. In the 1970s it was sold to the parish council and it remains in use as a parish hall. A new church hall, St Peter's Hall, was built just behind the church in 1977 and extended in 1979.

The most recent Rectors of Selsey have been Thomas Clayton Twitchell (1925-34), formerly Bishop of Polynesia, Robert Franklin (1934-44), George Henry Handisyde (1944-66), Hugh Pruen, who was Priest in Charge from 1966 to 1974, and Roger Walker (1974-81). The present incumbent is Rev. V. R. Cassam, who became Rector and Vicar in 1981; Selsey is one of very few livings where the same man holds both positions. The church is flourishing today with almost 300 on the electoral roll and an average of 150 people attending the main 10 a.m. communion service each Sunday. It is hoped that a new nave altar will be built in the near future as the present altar at the back of the chancel cannot be seen by a large proportion of the worshippers. St Peter's plays an active part in the life of the community with girl guides, brownies and rangers linked to the church and meeting in the church hall, as well as the Sunday School, church youth club, mothers' union and a mothers and toddlers group.

The Methodist Church

The parish church is not the only place of worship in Selsey today, though of course it was for many centuries. In 1815 William O'Bryan founded the Bible Christian denomination in the West Country. The sect rapidly gained adherents further east and the first Bible Christian chapel in Selsey is believed to have been built in 1835. A Sunday School was begun the following year. For some children, at work all week from a very early age, this would have offered them their only chance to learn to read and write. Two sessions were usually held each Sunday, from about 9.00 a.m. till noon, and again from 1.30 to 4.00 p.m. At that time there was no resident minister, but visiting Methodist ministers, members of a flourishing circuit based on Chichester, would have preached in the village. These men would have been poorly paid and badly housed, spending much of their time walking long distances in all weather to visit scattered societies and subject to ridicule and rough handling by hostile mobs. The 1851 Census for Selsey records a William Clarke, 'visitor' and Bible

Christian Minister born in Tavistock in Devon, as living in the High Street. Later, William Phillips, a lay preacher from West Wittering, used to conduct services in Selsey, preaching from a chair on the Green. Having inherited a substantial sum of money, he built the Fish Lane Chapel for his fellow worshippers, probably near the site of the present Chapel Cottage in East Street.

15. The Bible Christian church in the High Street. This photograph must have been taken between 1866 when the church was built and 1907 when it became a Methodist church. Note the thatched cottage to the south of the church which was destroyed by fire in 1925.

The church was a flourishing one. In May 1863 the Bible Christians in Selsey celebrated the 27th anniversary of their 'Sabbath School'. After special services on the Sunday, Monday was a gala day for the children who processed with banners through the village, singing. A picnic tea was provided for them after which they entertained the adults in the evening with a concert of singing and recitations. At that time the Sunday School had 130 children on its roll, instructed by 18 teachers. The Whit Monday procession was an important annual village event. In view of the number of children alone linked with the chapel, it is not surprising that within a few years the Fish Lane building was too small for the congregation. In 1866 a 'Barn and a Gate Room' was purchased for the Bible Christians by the Hon. Mrs. Vernon-Harcourt for £35. This was then demolished, and a larger chapel in the High Street was erected by Selsey's nonconformists in 1867. The east front (facing the street) is faced with squared knapped flints, and has white brick dressings and quoins. The building has narrow pointed lancet windows and was constructed in the 13th-century Gothic style.

The Bible Christians were very active at the end of the 19th century. There were frequent newspaper reports of bazaars, concerts and Sunday School anniversaries held at the chapel, and from the 1880s there was growing support for the temperance movement. This aimed to convince people of the evils of drink and the advantages of temperance or total abstinence. Converts were usually asked to sign the 'pledge', more formally the 'Abstaining Declaration', which read: 'I hereby agree to abstain from all Intoxicating Liquors as beverages and will endeavour to promote the objects of the Society'. When a branch of the White Ribbon Army was established in connection with the Selsey chapel in 1882, over 200 joined, a surprisingly high number at a time when the population of the village was very small. As a result, 'some who were much addicted to intemperance have been reformed and though not in the habit of attending the house of God previously, they are now regular in their attendance'. In January of the following year 150 people sat down to a temperance tea, over 100 being 'pledged abstainers'. In the evening a service of song was put on by the White Ribbon Army Choir and, at the close, six new pledges were taken. By 1887 the Bible Christians of Selsey also had a thriving Mutual Improvement Society. Its programme of debates and speakers helped in the training of preachers and teachers for local chapels.

In 1907 the Bible Christian, Methodist New Connexion and United Methodist Free Church denominations amalgamated, forming the United Methodist Church. Also in 1907 the chapel was extended. It was during these early years of the present century that the congregation increased sufficiently to warrant the appointment of a minister for the church who would reside in Selsey itself. The church was very active at that time and elderly folk still remember with pleasure special events such as Sunday School anniversaries and outings to Goodwood, carol singing all round the village, missionary teas, and rallies at the West Wittering chapel every Good Friday. In 1939 a large hall, Crossley Hall, was added, paid for by the Crossley family, manufacturers of engines for private and commercial vehicles, who lived in the village. This was put to good use soon afterwards as a canteen for troops training in the Selsey area, many from Canada and America. In 1977 the premises were further improved and modernised.

Until recently the Methodist church was the only Free Church in the village so that it drew newly-arrived members of other denominations, such as Baptists and Congregationalists, into its fellowship. Rev. F. R. Dowson was minister of the church from 1974 to 1987, when he was replaced by Rev. Roy Rabey who served for over 30 years in the Methodist Church in Zimbabwe. Today the church provides seating accommodation for nearly 150 people but this is often inadequate and additional chairs have to be brought in. There are 120 church members, but the community roll exceeds 400. Every Sunday during the summer season, the Methodist minister organised a service at the Pontins Broadreeds Centre.

St Wilfrid's Catholic Church

Reference has been made earlier to the apparently hostile attitude of the people of Selsey to Roman Catholicism. However, by the start of the present century at least, there was a substantial Catholic community in the village. Prior to 1916 Selsey Catholics went to Chichester for mass. Early in 1916 a Sunday evening service was held in Mrs. Satow's house in Manor Road and by August there was a regular Sunday mass in a room over the *Fisherman's Joy*, which was subsequently converted into a chapel. *The Universe*, a Catholic journal, reported on 26 July 1918 of the considerable anxiety caused to the Catholics of Selsey by the news that the *Fisherman's Joy* had changed hands and would no longer be let to them for services. Fortunately, new premises were secured and the previous Sunday mass had been said at the Scout Hall in the High Street, 'in the presence of a large and relieved congregation'.

The new concrete building, on land in Station Road given by Dr. André, was completed in 1919 and provided seating for 100 people. The first mass was offered in May 1919 and

16. St Wilfrid's Roman Catholic church, Church Road, in 1987.

the church officially opened in July. It was attended by clergy from Chichester who could travel to the village by means of the Selsey tram (*see* chapter ten) at a return cost of 1s. 6d., including bicycle. *Kelly's Directory* for 1927 states that St Wilfrid's Catholic church was served from St Richard's in South Street, Chichester, from June to September each year. This continued until 1953 when Father Delaney retired to Selsey and could spend more time caring for the Catholics of the village. There was a fire in the timber yard adjoining the church in 1928 which made extensive repairs necessary.

The present church of Our Lady of Mount Carmel and St Wilfrid, in Church Road, was built for £23,090 in 1961 of reconstituted Cotswold stone and was officially opened by Archbishop Cowderay in May 1962. In May 1970 that part of the Manhood peninsula comprising Selsey, Sidlesham, the Witterings, Birdham and Itchenor became a parish in its own right, separate from Chichester. Father Vincent-Maxwell was appointed the first parish priest. The present presbytery was completed in 1972 by Father Campbell Price and is the home of the current priest, the Very Rev. Canon Patrick Cox. The church today serves a community of some 250 parishioners, rising to 400 during the summer, and a church hall was built during 1986.

East Beach Evangelical Church

East Beach Evangelical Church, a modern timber-framed building, overlaid with render and brick, is situated in Marisfield Place next to the East Beach shopping centre. It was built in the early 1980s to serve the large number of new residents coming to live at East Beach. A spacious recreation room was provided upstairs for youth work and this can double as a balcony for the main church when congregations are large. The church was built by members themselves and is a testimony to the faith of the original congregation. It is an inter-denominational and independent church, with simple bible-based services, and serves all age groups by means of a Sunday School, family services, youth clubs, women's meetings and senior citizens' teas.

All four of these churches work closely together and the ecumenical movement is alive and well in Selsey. There is, for example, a united carol service every Christmas, held at each of the churches in turn.

Chapter Seven

Selsey and the Sea

Wrecks, Wrecking and Smuggling

The question of profits arising from wreckage cast up on the shore of Selsey Bill has been a burning one from the earliest times. St Wilfrid's arrival in Selsey at the time of the famine and drought was not his first visit to the area. Twenty years earlier, the ship on which he was travelling from Compiègne after his consecration as bishop in Paris[17] was wrecked off the peninsula and he fell into the hands of the natives of Selsey. His chaplain, Eddius Stephanus, recorded:

> For a great gale blowing from the South-east, the swelling waves threw them on the unknown coast of the South Saxons . . . And the heathen coming with a great army intended to seize the ship, to divide the spoil of money, to take them captive forthwith and to put to the sword such as resisted. To whom our great Bishop spoke gently and peaceably . . . But they with stern and cruel hearts . . . would not let these people of the Lord go, saying proudly that 'All that the sea threw on the land became as much theirs as their own property'.

There are many records of wrecked ships and of wreckage washed ashore and claimed by the lords of the manor of Selsey. One of the earliest, reported by a Commission of Inquiry, was of 'a ship called "La Seinte Marie de Port Valet" of Spain . . . freighted with wine for England . . . driven by a storm on a rock off the Island of Seleseye, and partly broken up, and seventy-one tuns of wine, chests, plates of iron, swords and other goods were taken as wreck by men of the island'. Henry VI had specifically granted to Bishop Adam Moleyns that the lands of Chichester Cathedral should be exempt from the jurisdiction of the Court of Admiralty in the matter of wrecks. This was confirmed in a deed of exchange of 1562, when among the grants made to the See in return for the manor was *wrecca maris* (wrecks of the sea). Bishops did claim wreckage in practice as well as in theory. For example, in 1586 and 1587 cotton and beef respectively were taken from ships wrecked on the bishop's land and in 1591 it was decreed in the Court of Arches that 'neither the said reverend father nor his successors or tenants, servants or ministers should from that time be arrested or molested in any way as to the wrecks in the manors and lands of the said See'.

The Court Rolls are full of references to wreckage of boats and other flotsam and jetsam, all claimed 'without dispute' by the bailiff of the lord of the manor. Considerable quantities of wine and whisky were carried dutifully to the lord, but in April 1615 John Sturt and John Turkett each found a barrel of whisky and concealed them in their barns, for which they were fined 40s. and 10s. respectively. In the Court of Sir William Morley in October 1688, it was recorded that 'a small pinnace had come ashore as wreck and was saved by certain tenants . . . and this small pinnace, according to the custom of the Manor, belonged of right to the Lord of the Manor'. Salving of wrecks was an important industry on the peninsula. But endings were not always happy. *The Chichester Observer* reported in December 1910 the death of a fisherman, John Arnell, and his five-year-old nephew, Alfred Charles Arnell, who had drowned while trying to bring ashore casks seen floating in the sea off the fishing beach. A verdict of death by misadventure was recorded – the casks had been too heavy for a small boat in rough seas.

The same people keen to make a profit from wrecks may also have been involved in smuggling. The contraband trade was practically extinct by the 20th century, but had been active in Sussex in earlier centuries. Silks and other French goods were smuggled into the Selsey area during the wars against France in Queen Anne's reign. The *Sussex Weekly Advertiser* and *Lewes Journal* used to be full of advertisements for the sale of seized goods at the Customs Houses. In one newspaper edition in March 1789 no less than 12,372 gallons of spirits captured at Selsey were advertised for sale by the Crown, proof of the scale of operations. Most citizens, however law-abiding, have always felt a certain shamefaced sympathy with smuggling and piracy. When a butcher informed against John Reeves, the miller at Selsey, the villagers attacked his home and burned him in effigy. There is even a tradition in Selsey that some of the Rectors used to take a 'tithe of kegs' and that an underground passage led from the old Rectory to the Mound. In the Middle Ages wool was regularly smuggled out of Selsey and Chichester harbours and Flemish cloth smuggled in. In 1336 the bailiffs of Chichester and 13 other ports were ordered to prevent the trade. In fact 'owling', the smuggling *out* of wool, continued into the first quarter of the 19th century.

Selsey had considerable natural advantages as a centre for smuggling. The tidal estuaries which form Chichester and Pagham harbours provided sheltered and secluded landing sites, and the tide race through the narrow entrances could be used to carry in rafts of floating tubs. In addition there were excellent open shores in the vicinity, partially sheltered by the Isle of Wight. The fact that Selsey was still cut off from the mainland in the 18th century also made it a natural landing site as the enforcement of law and order there was particularly difficult. Much common land remained unenclosed until the early 19th century and the commons interspersed with the open fields behind Selsey were ideal for the concealment of contraband. At the height of the trade in wool around 1720, a skipper from Selsey was taking a vessel to France and back every week and a local farmer was said to have made £10,000 profit in six years of part-time operations, perhaps driving the smuggled goods to and from the boats.

In 1748/9 Mr. William Galley, a Customs House officer at Southampton, and Mr. Daniel Chater, a shoemaker, were savagely murdered by 14 notorious local smugglers. They were associates of the well-organised Hawkhurst Gang, active in Kent and Sussex. In 1747 a cargo of brandy, tea and rum which they had smuggled over from Guernsey on their vessel the *Three Brothers* was captured at Poole. The crew escaped and the gang later attacked Poole Customs House to recover the goods which they regarded as their property, forcing the doors open with hatchets. One of the gang was captured some months later and the murders were committed to prevent evidence being given against the other smugglers. Both men were tortured and then Galley was buried alive in a shallow grave and Chater was thrown down a well and large stones were hurled on to his mutilated body. Seven smugglers were tried and executed in Chichester and two, John Cobby of Sidlesham and John Hammond of Bersted, were hung in Chichester and their bodies subsequently hung in chains 'on Selsey Isle, on the high ground or heath where they sometimes landed their smuggled goods'.[18] We cannot be certain of the precise location of the gibbet but, on the tithe map of 1839, part of Hill Field on which Beacon House stood used to be called Gibbet Field. This was high ground so may have been the site of a gibbet on which smugglers were hung to warn passing shipping of the fate in store for anyone daring to cheat the 'Revenuers'.

The saloon bar of the *Lifeboat Inn* at the end of Albion Road still exhibits modern facsimiles of posters offering substantial rewards for the apprehension of smugglers who were active on the Selsey peninsula every night that the moon and tides were right. The peak of smuggling was in the 18th century and tobacco, tea and spirits were the main items of contraband. In East Street, near the *Fisherman's Joy*, is an old house still called 'Smugglers Cottage' and there are many other houses, including some in the High Street, with smugglers' cupboards in their lofts. A smugglers' tunnel is believed to have run from below the Malt

17. Etching of the 1747 raid on the Poole Customs House.

House down to the fishing beach. The Methodists strongly opposed smuggling and Wesley refused to have as a member of his societies any person connected with this illegal traffic. In 1836 the conversion of a notorious smuggler in Selsey infused new life into the small Methodist (Bible Christian) society there. After 1822 the coastguard service worked for the prevention of smuggling, patrolling the beaches and cliff tops. Drastic reductions in import duties by Peel's government in the 1840s made smuggling less profitable, and by 1850 it had virtually died away.

Fishing in Selsey

An important feature of Selsey even today is its fishing community. Selsey has enjoyed a considerable reputation for its fish ever since St Wilfrid's time, particularly for its cockles. Camden wrote of Selsey in 1586, '. . . now it is most famous for good cockles and full lobsters', and Izaak Walton wrote in 1653, '. . . there are four good things in Sussex, a Selsey cockle, a Chichester lobster, an Arundel mullet, and an Amberley trout'. Selsey's cockles were mainly gathered in Pagham Harbour in earlier centuries and the closing of the harbour in 1873 (*see* page 45) led to a great reduction in the trade.

The collection of oysters in the area goes back at least to Roman times, oyster shells having been discovered within the Mound at Norton. Selsey oysters are rich in common pearls. After Kent and the Thames estuary, the Chichester Harbour area has always been the main centre of Britain's native oyster trade. At one time oysters were artificially

18. Fishermen's Beach in 1935, showing neat rows of lobster pots.

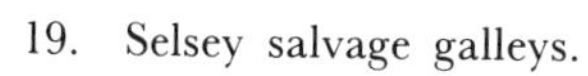

19. Selsey salvage galleys.

cultivated – Heron-Allen knew of some disused oyster pans or beds between the Windmill Path and Medmerry Farm, probably on the site of the mill pond of the old Selsey tidal mill.

Selsey fishermen caught a wide variety of fish at the turn of the century including herring, pollack, skate, cod, ray, mackerel, bass, bream, flounder, mullet, whiting, hake, plaice, dab, whelks, lobsters, crabs, prawns and oysters. At that time there was a fleet of 21 large fishing boats (2½ to 6 tons) and 23 smaller boats working regularly from Selsey. The Board of Agriculture and Fisheries supplied the following statistics relating to the quantity and value of wet and shell fish landed at Selsey in 1909: 377 cwt. of wet fish valued at £566; 159,290 crabs valued at £5,308; 38,036 lobsters valued at £1,902; 62,000 oysters valued at £248; and 1,426 cwt. of other shellfish worth £1,744. All this fish had to be carted by road to Chichester Station before the arrival of the Selsey tram in 1897. The crabs and lobsters caught off Selsey tend to be smaller than the average but in June 1936 *The West Sussex Gazette* reported that a Selsey fisherman had caught a 10 lb. salmon off the Bill and in 1938 four fishermen had a record catch of four tons of bass when fishing in Pagham Harbour. The fish weighed up to 10 and 12 pounds apiece and were caught using the Seine method of netting. The men rowed backwards and forwards from Pagham to Selsey where lorries were waiting to take the fish to Billingsgate, Brighton and Portsmouth. Much earlier, in 1883, a bottle whale had been caught and was transported, wrapped in wet blankets, to Brighton Aquarium. Freak conditions must have prevailed that year because a few months later fishermen saw a score of flying fish rise out of the sea near Selsey, pursued by an albatross, something not even the oldest fisherman of the time could remember.

Crab and lobster pots or 'creels' are perhaps the most prominent feature of the 'fishermen's beach' on the east shore of the Selsey peninsula. In the past these were all made of twigs of the golden willow, each fisherman making his own pots using locally-grown osiers, though by the turn of the century it had become necessary to import twigs from Holland and Belgium. In 1883 a silver medal was awarded to Charles Perrin of Selsey at the International Fisheries Exhibition 'for his superior skill in fishpot making', his wickerwork being classified as 'first class'.

A fisherman's life is never easy. In earlier centuries fishermen were in danger of being molested or captured by foreign enemies, privateers or pirates. As late as the 17th century, Dutch privateers off Selsey took some small vessels and prevented other fishing boats from going to sea. Many examples of death by drowning can be found in the parish registers: '17 July 1802, John Stevenson, 66, drowned at fishing' and '30 January 1804, James Fifield, 21, and John Walker, drowned near the Bill'. A gale in March 1818 destroyed the entire fleet of Selsey fishing boats. A public subscription was opened to raise money to replace the vessels and assist families in distress.[19]

During the 19th century and at the start of the present, the Selsey fishermen jointly owned and operated 'the galley', a long boat powered by 22 oarsmen, 11 on each side. Galley boats operated before the first lifeboat was stationed in Selsey, but after 1861 would go to sea at the same time as the lifeboat and, after any rescue work was complete, the 'pilot' of the galley would bargain with the captain of the damaged or stranded vessel and agree the cost of piloting her to a safe harbour. In March 1862, for example, *The West Sussex Gazette and County Advertiser* recorded a galley going out to a vessel washed on to a shoal off Selsey Bill. In 1882 there were two galleys, appropriately named the *Rescue* and the *Friend*. The galley represented a profitable, though risky, way for the fishermen to supplement their meagre incomes. The galley co-operative was disbanded in the 1930s when larger powered vessels began sailing in waters out of reach of the man-powered galley.

In the 1841 census 12 of the 20 men living in the aptly-named Fish Lane were listed as fishermen and a large proportion of the entire male population of the village earned their

20. Selsey fishermen around the 1890s.

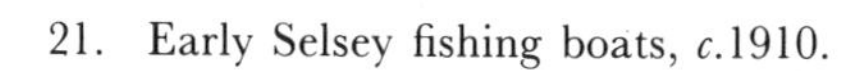

21. Early Selsey fishing boats, *c.*1910.

living from the sea, including boys of 15 and men of 80 years of age. By the early years of the present century there were over 100 Selsey men employed in the fishing industry, owning some 20 smacks and 30 small boats. They sold their fish to a merchant on the spot, who would distribute them among the fishmongers of the coastal and inland towns. For ordinary dinner-table fish, the people of Selsey rely on London and Grimsby! In the past anyone could build himself a 'fish shop', a tarred hut in which a fisherman would keep his gear and for which he paid a rent of 10s. a year to the lord of the manor. In 1907 a builder began erecting a residential bungalow on the fishermen's beach. The fishermen pulled it down and then repeated their act of defiance on another bungalow. They claimed to have a statutory title to the land by undisturbed possession extending over many generations. In 1909 the situation was resolved, largely through the mediation of Rev. Cavis-Brown (whose role in establishing the rights of the fishermen is commemorated on a plaque in St Peter's church) – a charter defined certain land on the shore which was to be used by the fishermen for drawing up their boats, storing lobster pots and tackle, drying and

22. The *Fisherman's Joy* around the turn of the century when Walter Arnell Smith was proprietor. The men standing below the fascinating advertisement on the side wall are coastguard officers. The building dates back to the early 19th century.

mending nets, but for no other purpose. They were entitled to use the huts already erected for those purposes, but not for residence. Subject to these rights of the fishermen, the land was to be reserved as an open area for public benefit. The owners of existing huts were to pay 5s. a year for them, and the size and position of future huts were to be controlled. In February 1909 the owners of residential bungalows on the fishing beach were evicted.

Fishing continues to be the staple industry in Selsey today, directly employing about 100 men and women, the majority working on the fishing boats but some in the storage tanks on East Beach and others on the maintenance of engines and vessels. Selsey's oldest fisherman is Willie Arnell, better known as 'Honest Bill'. Now 75 years of age, he has been fishing off the Selsey coast since he was nine. The bulk of the catches are of shellfish, though wet fish catches are now on the increase. The average size boat used by the modern fishermen is about 35 ft. and such boats can often be seen anchored at sea opposite the fishermen's huts on East Beach. Fishermen today are very concerned about a massive bank of shingle building up on the east side of the peninsula which is slowly moving west towards the Bill. Mooring space for boats is becoming limited and the men cannot sail in or out two hours either side of low water on a spring tide. The Selsey Lobster Co. on Kingsway does a flourishing trade in crabs, whelks, cockles and prawns. The company's director is Mr. B. J. Arrow and for the last 20 years or so his family has marketed most of the fish caught in the Selsey area, all of it being exported to specialist markets throughout the world. Before that time, all fish was sold off the beach or to Billingsgate Market in London. A substantial business has been built up in Church Road which manufactures and supplies lobster pots to local fishermen and others throughout the country.

Every August the Selsey fishermen race their boats in the 'Crabbers Race', re-introduced in 1979. This event was inaugurated in the 1870s as the Selsey Regatta. It continued into the 1930s apart from the years 1914-18, but ceased to be held regularly after the Second World War. Originally, sailing boats would have been raced but today the fishing boats are driven by powerful engines, so all entries are carefully handicapped according to their performance the previous year. The 4½-mile course is laid out opposite East Beach, the boats racing for a much-coveted shield. There is also keen competition to win the prize for best decorated boat. In 1980 all proceeds from the event were used to purchase *Sealion*, a fast inshore lifeboat, urgently needed in Selsey. The village is full of reminders of the prominent part fishing has played throughout its history: Fisherman's Walk, the *Fisherman's Joy* public house and, in Albion Road, an early 19th-century flint and brick house called 'Fishers Cottage'.

Pagham (or Selsey) Harbour

Pagham Harbour is a comparatively recent geographical term. Until the start of the 19th century the area was known as Selsey Harbour and in fact four-fifths of the harbour lies within the boundaries of the parish of Selsey. From the earliest times, attempts had been made to reclaim the harbour from the sea and convert it into pastureland through the erection of dykes. Throughout the centuries, reclaimed land was the subject of bitter lawsuits concerning ownership. As early as 1664, Sir John Denham and his son-in-law Sir William Morley, Lord of the Manor of Selsey, petitioned the Crown for leave to reclaim the harbour. An investigation was made and in 1665 reported:

> it contains . . . 1,300 acres of ground lying between the Isle of Selsey, and the Maine Land of Sussex, there being a small isthmus or beach of stone, cast up by the sea, at the west end of the said island there, joining it to the maine land, but at the easte end the sea comes in by a channell of about twelve perches broad at low water, and about twenty perches at high water, between the said island

> and maine land . . . the rest of the ground all slubb, dirt, and in many places, sandy . . . there may be about nine hundred acres improved . . . by making a great sea-wall, or damm at the said east end.

The commission recommended reclamation, stating that 900 acres would be dry and fit for tillage within three years. In fact no such reclamation took place at this time and the parish registers in the 17th and 18th centuries continue to report the burial of persons 'drowned at the ferry'.

Between 1805 and 1809 Sir James Peachey (Baron Selsey since 1794) was responsible for the construction of a strong bank about 1,500 ft. long on the site of the old Wadeway or Ferry. As a result, 312 acres of land were reclaimed from the sea and became usable farmland. In 1852 a detailed survey was made of the harbour on the authority of the Harbour Department of the Admiralty. At that time it was 1¾ miles long by 1¾ miles broad at its greatest extent and contained an area of almost 800 acres. The harbour was then still used for trade; 68 vessels entered it each year, carrying an average of 25 tons each, usually coal and grain which was taken to Sidlesham Mill (tidal), and flour which was taken out from the mill. It is interesting to note that, according to the Armada survey of 1587, ships of 40 tons had then been able to navigate up to Sidlesham Mill, proof that the harbour was gradually silting up. The 1852 report advocated closing up the harbour and reclaiming the enclosed land, by means of a sea wall. For 20 years after this report nothing was done, but in 1873 an Act was passed 'to Authorise the Construction of Works and Reclamation of Lands in Pagham Harbour'. Under this Act, a company was formed to construct an embankment or sea wall 407 yards long from near the old coastguard house at Pagham to Selsey Beach. £36,000 was supplied for the work and the company had the power to borrow a further £10,000. Part of the reclaimed land, after drainage, was to belong to the Crown but some would belong to the company. The Crown land, some 318 acres, was sold to Mr. Frederick William Grafton in 1877; he purchased the Manor of Selsey in 1878 and the reclaimed land passed down with the Manor through successive generations. For nearly 40 years the rich alluvial mud of the reclaimed harbour yielded good crops of corn and barley on the eastern side and supported a large head of cattle which grazed on the lush meadowland to the west.

Selsey has always been liable to flooding. Rev. Barré Phipps often recorded flooding in the parish registers in the early 19th century: 'Sunday, October 22nd, 1820, the day after the full moon, the wind, being south and south-west, a remarkably high tide, accompanied by a violent wind, burst over the shingle bank of the sea, over the sea-wall, maintained by the Rector and by Mr. George Copis, covered entirely the marsh belonging to both of them and flowed into the farmyard of the Rector.' It is no wonder that this particular Rector spent many years on the Continent, with the permission of the Bishop, on account of his wife's health, which suffered 'from the cold and marshy nature of the climate of Selsey'.

The most memorable flooding took place on 16 December 1910 when the sea broke through the harbour wall, demolishing a 40-yard stretch. During the previous week the entire south coast had been ravaged by storms, with torrential rain and gale-force winds blowing from the south-west. The great inundation which took place on that day flooded almost 5,000 acres of pasture and submerged the Selsey tram line to the south of Sidlesham. Even the main road from Chichester to Selsey, raised some feet above the level of the low-lying land, was under water for hundreds of yards at high tide. Haystacks were submerged and men had to go out in boats to help livestock swim to safety. The mill and some houses were flooded but, miraculously, there was no loss of life. The gasworks were flooded which meant no light for the village and a special supply of lamps, oil and candles had to be rushed in from Chichester. Selsey experienced Christmas 1910 in darkness. This story

23. The flooded station and mill at Sidlesham, December 1910.

24. Children enjoying the flood water near Sidlesham mill, December 1910. This tidal mill was pulled down *c.*1913, having become redundant when the harbour was closed. The foundations of the mill can be seen today just west of the *Crab and Lobster Inn.*

naturally reached the national newspapers and the *Daily News* reported on 19 December that:

> since Friday, Selsey has been an island in the English Channel. For a distance of five miles, from the southern corner of Bracklesham Bay on the west, to Pagham on the east, the sea now rolls unchecked, save for a solitary dyke, some 20ft. in thickness, which forms the only means of communication between the 1,200[20] inhabitants of Selsey Village and the City of Chichester upon the mainland. Between 4,000 and 5,000 acres of pasture have been submerged, three farmhouses and several cottages have narrowly escaped destruction . . . Add to this the fact that the light railway between Chichester and Selsey has two miles of its track under deep water, and it will be seen that the catastrophe is of no mean proportion.

This calamity brought home the futility of all man's efforts in the face of the power of nature and the sea. An old Selsey fisherman living in Sidlesham remarked after this great

25. More recent flood damage in Selsey, in December 1951. On the night of 28 December winds reached 100 m.p.h. and the sea broke through the shingle bank and flowed inland, making the headlines in national newspapers. East Beach was worst hit and bungalows in Manor Lane were flooded to a depth of three or four feet. All the residents were evacuated to the *Selsey Hotel*. Electricity supplies were cut off for a day and part of Broadreeds camp was swept away. The men in the photograph include George and Eric Woodland, and Ken Maidment.

26. & 27. The lifeboat station in 1928 and 1954 respectively. These two photographs graphically reveal the speed at which the sea erodes the coastline of the Selsey peninsula. The damage to the centre portion of the walkway in the 1954 picture was caused by an American landing craft which slipped its mooring in a gale in 1947.

flood, 'Man drove the fish away from Sidlesham, and, you see, God has brought them back!' Considerable damage was caused to boats and houses by further flooding in December 1911 and March 1912: some bungalows were lifted from their foundations and, in one case, furniture completely washed out through the windows. Much later, during Christmas week in 1951, gales again threatened the complete destruction of Selsey. A writer to *The Sussex County Magazine* in February 1952 expressed amazement that people should continue to live on sites close to the shore, ignoring the known facts of coastal erosion and the inevitability of storm damage, and then demand enormous expenditure on coastal defences which would not last more than a few years. He stated that as long as English weather and the English Channel remained unchanged, human effort could not amount to much against them.

It was in the 1950s that it became obvious that improvements would have to be made to Selsey's coastal defences because the low cliffs, and the land mass of brick earth, shingle, gravel and sand offered little resistance to the waves. Another writer to *The Sussex County Magazine* in September 1955 reminded readers that the current lifeboat house was built on land at the end of Albion Road in 1923. By the time he was writing, it could only be reached by a footbridge over the sea, more that 300 yards long. He claimed that no less than 34 acres of land had been lost in the previous 18 years from a mile of beach, giving Selsey the dubious distinction of having lost more land per yard of frontage than any other place in the British Isles in the 20th century. Each winter more and more houses and bungalows disappeared, including some of architectural importance like Beacon House which had been a boarding house south of where Pontins Holiday Camp is today, and was washed away by the sea in the early 1920s.

Eventually Chichester Rural District Council prepared a scheme to protect the land. It would cost an estimated £360,000 to build the necessary sea walls and groynes. An Exchequer grant was obtained for phase one, the protection of West Beach, and this was completed in 1954. Phase two, defences for the gale-battered East Beach, was delayed by negotiations over finance, but in April 1955 the government agreed to make a grant of £79,000 towards the cost. Selsey was protected from the following winter's gales by strong sea walls, still standing today. Every winter the village fishermen have to repair and improve these defences – the struggle against the sea is never ending. Compensation under an Act of 1949 was paid to people whose homes were washed away. One expert in the 1950s made an amusing reference to Canute in this context: 'The only compensation he got was wet feet, and I think that is the only compensation people *should* get if they build beside the foreshore!'. Since the 1950s these walls have proved inadequate to withstand the force of the winter seas. In many places the defences are crumbling and it is possible that, unless improvements are made soon, a surge of high water could break through and more land might be lost for ever. Work to control the flow of water at the entrance to Pagham Harbour began in September 1987. This month was chosen in order to minimise the disturbance to the colony of rare little terns nesting in the harbour. The £435,000 project, being carried out by the Southern Water Authority, will ensure the continued success of the drainage of some 5,400 acres of low-lying land surrounding the harbour and will protect the unique harbour nature reserve, an overwintering area for 120 species of birds.

Selsey as a Holiday Resort

There have been many attempts to 'develop' Selsey as a seaside resort. In 1887, for example, plans were drawn up at County Hall, Lewes, for an Act of Parliament to be entitled the 'Selsey Railway and Pier Act', which would authorise the construction of a railway from Chichester to Selsey and a pier, 100 yards long, from the high water mark near to where

Beacon House once stood. Nothing came of this plan, but the opening of the Selsey tramway in 1897 made it easier for visitors to get to the then unspoiled fishing village. The tramway was extended right down to the beach in 1898, but no regular service ran on it after 1905.

As early as July 1907 *The Daily Mail* was promoting Selsey as a haven for summer visitors: 'The rector and vicar of Selsey states that his parishioners live to an average age of 75. It is not astonishing. It is only amazing that they do not live to the average age of 100.' Selsey was recommended as the place 'where the sun shines', where rainfall is below average, with the sea on three sides giving sands for children and safe, clean bathing, and the protection of a natural submerged breakwater for yachts. It was also recommended for its fresh fish and lobsters, the birds and wildlife at Pagham Harbour and for its proximity to the ancient city of Chichester. Its fine sea views, from Beachy Head to the Needles, were a great attraction, too, especially for those interested in watching fleet manoeuvres in the Solent. Selsey drew great crowds in 1887, keen to observe the fleet at Queen Victoria's Jubilee Review and to see the huge celebration bonfire lit on the Bill which was visible for many miles both on land and sea.

In November 1904 the following verse, in appreciation of Selsey's attractions, was published in *The West Sussex Gazette*:

> Where tired men and women come
> From busy towns awhile;
> Where faces showing weariness
> Soon brighten up and smile,
> Where children paddle, dip and dig
> Throughout the summer's hours;
> Where quaint old houses, snuggly thatched,
> Look neat with shrubs and flowers,
> Where all around so restful is,
> By sea-shore, field, or lane;
> Where breeze from spacious sea or land
> Invigorates again!

More tangible proof of Selsey's appeal is that as early as 1865 a Selsey Bill Club was founded in Clapham for the express purpose of making excursions to the village. A party of about 40 Londoners visited Selsey in June 1905, making their headquarters at the *New Inn* where they ate dinner and tea. The day was such a success that the club decided to arrange another excursion to Selsey for the last Sunday in August, to which ladies were to be invited as well as men.

In July 1907 Selsey on Sea Ltd. issued a share prospectus, hoping to sell 180,000 shares at £1 each. The company was formed for the purpose of acquiring and developing Selsey as a seaside resort. The company bought nearly 2,500 acres of land in the parishes of Selsey, Sidlesham, Pagham, North Mundham and East Wittering. In promoting Selsey as a worthwhile investment, it stated that in the village 'the average death-rate for the last five years was 8.8 per 1,000, whilst that of England and Wales for 10 years prior to the last census was 18.2 per 1,000'. The company had great plans for the development of Selsey.

> It is proposed to arrange for the erection of a Pier on the Eastern side of the Estate, so that pleasure steamers plying along the South Coast may be able to call at all states of the tide. The Estate will be laid out so as to leave sufficient land between the building sites and the beach to allow for a Marine Drive 80 feet wide, and a grass esplanade from 120 feet to 200 feet wide, which will be over three miles in length . . . The Northern portion of the Estate [just south-east of Sidlesham station] can be easily utilised for the construction of a Motor Track.

Perhaps it is as well that most of these plans never became reality!

Selsey was selective in the type of visitor it tried to attract. *The Chichester Observer* reported in May 1908:

28. Selsey Beach in the 1890s.

29. An early postcard of Selsey Beach from the Cynicus Publishing Co. Ltd.

> The beauty of Selsey as a holiday resort is its freedom from noisy trippers and the less desirable of the beach attractions . . . No, Selsey is not so keen on your London tripper. It prefers to enjoy the patronage of those people who go there just because it is not a modernised resort. It is its 'old-fashioned' charm which recommends it to those whose tastes do not call for Christy Minstrels, swing-boats, and steam roundabouts. Selsey is satisfied with lesser and more sober attractions. It possesses everything essential to wholesome pleasure and exercise.

30. The *Marine Hotel, c.*1925. The building was burnt down in about 1958.

Selsey's hotels catered well for their summer visitors from an early date. In January 1908 *The West Sussex Gazette* reported that the licence of the *Marine Hotel* had been transferred from Mr. J. B. Beattie to Mr. H. A. Cappelli. It described the splendid views of the sea from that establishment and explained that visitors had an absolute right to the foreshore up to Selsey Bill, so that there was safe bathing for children. A spacious saloon bar was

31a. The *Selsey Hotel* with the station building in the background on the far right, *c.*1920. The hotel is now called the *Star Gazer*.

31b. Advertisement for the *Selsey Hotel*, *c.*1910.

Telegrams—Selsey Hotel. Telephone—No. 17.

THE SELSEY HOTEL,

(OUTSIDE STATION),

SELSEY BILL,

Near Station, Sea and Golf Links. **CHICHESTER.**

Fine Lawns, Croquet and Tennis Courts.

Billiard Saloon and Motor Garage.

Proprietor—Mr. J. DAVIS.

also being constructed for guests. Sadly, the *Marine Hotel* was burnt to the ground in 1958 and has now been replaced by a residential estate known as Marine Park. In May 1912 a bowling green was opened at the *Selsey Hotel*, with a specially-arranged match against players from Chichester and tea in the grounds of the hotel. In 1916 Mr. J. Davis, proprietor, made considerable structural improvements to this hotel, realising that profit could be made from the growing prosperity and popularity of Selsey. The coffee room and lounge were extended, creating a dining room capable of accommodating almost 100 guests. There were splendid views of the sea from the hotel and visitors could relax on the lawn or the tennis courts. As can be seen, the hotel was advertised as the nearest to the golf links and the station. The *Selsey Hotel* was renamed the *Star Gazer* in 1970 in honour of Selsey's most famous resident, astronomer Patrick Moore, who lives in a charming 17th-century thatched house in West Street.

During the First World War Selsey, like most other south coast resorts, welcomed an unusually large number of visitors, 'the majority of the better class' according to *The Chichester Observer* in August 1915. There were even royal visitors occasionally – in July 1923 Prince George motored down to Selsey with friends and called in at the *Marine Hotel*, and in September 1929 the Prince of Wales (later Edward VIII) drove to East Beach with a party of friends for a picnic. Apparently only a few people on the beach recognised him.

In the 1920s sand competitions were held for children on Selsey beach, a first prize of £2 being given in 1927. These were organised by *The Daily Mail* on the nearest spring tide weekend to the August Bank Holiday. Throughout the 1920s complaints were made by local residents about the shortage of car parking facilities for day trippers and the consequent congestion in the village in the summer. In June 1928, however, Selsey's first public car park was opened, about a mile from the end of Marine Drive. A fee of 1s. was charged for a car for the whole day and overflow parking to accommodate 40 cars was available to the east of Bill House. The parks were organised by the Selsey Estates and managed by Messrs. Wyatt and Sons. The sea front was to be kept free of parked cars.

Broadreeds Holiday Camp, later Pontins Camp, was first mentioned in *Kelly's Directory* in the 1930s, as was Mill Farm Camping and Caravan Site, with J. and D. J. Wakely as proprietors. In the early days there were problems with the sanitary arrangements at the camping sites at Medmerry and Mill Lane. Many converted buses were used for accommodation as well as tents and caravans, and the number of latrines available were totally inadequate in August when there were hundreds of campers. Most visitors to Selsey in the first half of the present century would best remember the East Beach area with its holiday bungalows. It is surprisingly little altered today: many roads are still not made-up and a number of converted railway carriages can still be seen, giving the whole area the colourful appearance of an improvised shanty town. In the early 1930s Mr. J. A. Simonds bought Broadreed House (now claimed by the sea) and an adjoining field and by 1934 Broadreeds was advertising itself in a national newspaper[21] as 'Entirely brick-built, on the edge of the sands. Hot and Cold Water in All Bedrooms . . . Restaurant, Dance Hall . . . 47/6 per week, July 50/-, August 52/6. Special Whitsun terms 25/-'. Throughout the first decades of the present century the number of boarding houses, guest houses, apartments, tea rooms and restaurants in the village had been increasing rapidly, indicating a rise in the number of holidaymakers in Selsey. In 1962 Broadreeds, until then a family concern, was bought up by Pontins Camp Ltd.

Selsey 'took off' as a tourist resort in the 1930s, when more and more people owned cars and wished to spend a few weeks in the summer by the sea. From that time until 1958, when West Sussex County Council's first town plan for Selsey was finally approved, development almost got out of hand. Selsey's caravan sites were among the largest in the country and

32. Medmerry Farm camp in 1933 with the windmill in the background. This semi-rural scene with haystacks and barns is very different from today's huge caravan park.

33. Park Lane, East Beach, in 1938. This area of Selsey has changed surprisingly little over the intervening half century.

34. Broadreeds holiday camp from the air in 1949. The light strip to the right of the chalets was probably mustard, grown regularly on this land which belonged to Ralph Selsby. There are now fears that houses may be built on the site of the camp which would end archaeologists' chances of a full-scale excavation of the area, possibly part of an Iron Age settlement.

35. An aerial view of the village in 1960 when caravans were popular holiday residences. The fields east of the High Street are today criss-crossed by roads such as Wellington Gardens, Dennys Close and Malthouse Road. Note the water tower off School Lane in the top left hand corner of the picture and St Peter's church (top right), still surrounded by trees rather than houses.

summer populations expanded too rapidly for services such as water and sewerage to cope with.

Today a wide range of hotels, guest houses and caravan parks cater for summer visitors, up to 15,000 a week during the height of the season, an astonishing number considering the fact that Selsey's total resident population is only about 10,000. Pontins recently underwent a two-year improvement plan costing over £2,000,000. Improvements included a dining room seating 1,100 visitors at any one time, central heating in guests' rooms during the winter months, and a heated swimming pool, sauna and solarium. Selsey has certainly moved with the times. The holiday camp is nevertheless to close at the end of 1988 and Selsey parish council is considering leasing or purchasing some of the buildings for a sports complex. It is most likely, however, that houses will be built on the site, off Grafton Road.

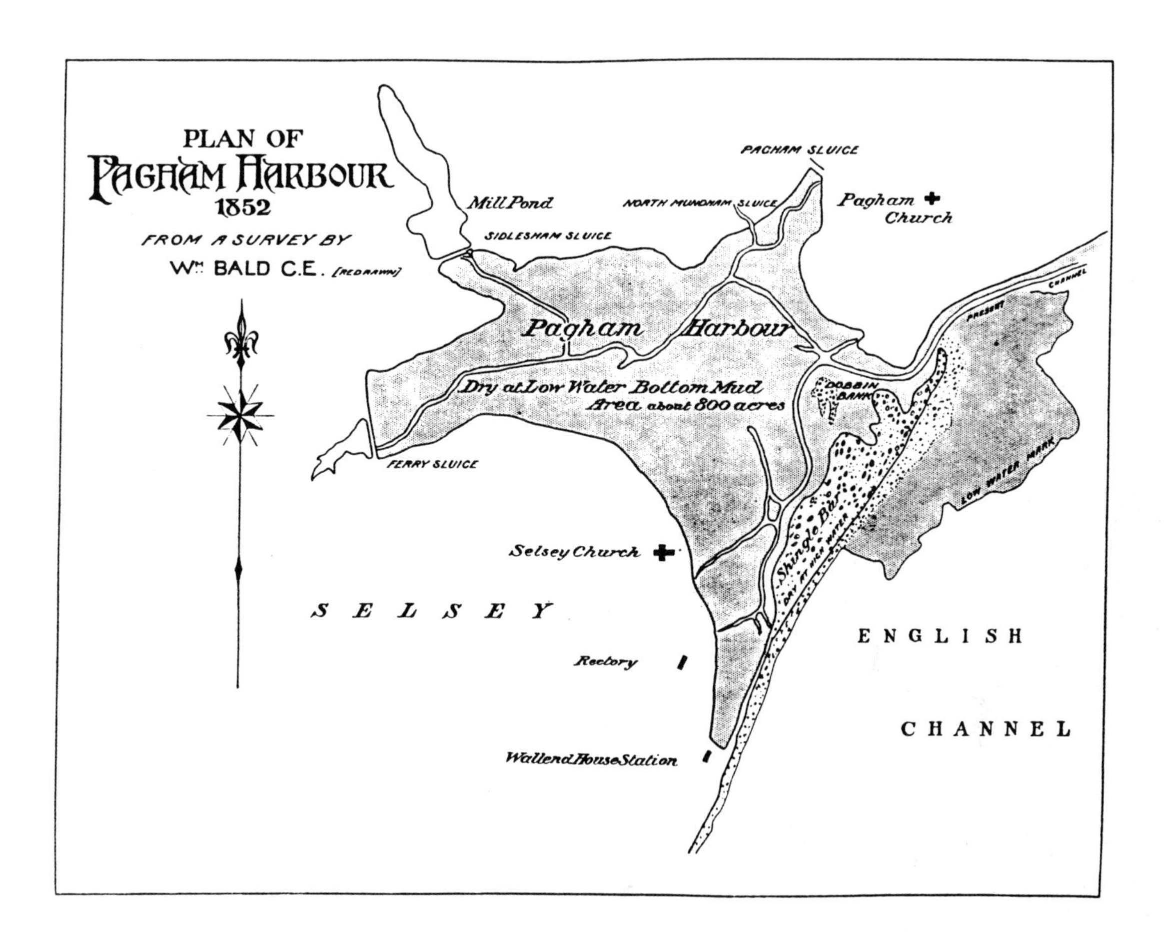

Chapter Eight

Emergency and Public Services

Selsey Lifeboats

Selsey has had a lifeboat since 1861 when the National Lifeboat Institute stationed *The Friend* (so named because the Society of Friends made a generous donation of £200 towards the cost of this boat) on the beach there to provide hope for all those sailing past the treacherous Owers Bank and Mixon Rocks just off Selsey Bill, which have claimed many lives over the centuries. Until then, with the exception of two vessels recently placed on the Isle of Wight, there had been no lifeboat between Worthing and Lyme Regis in Dorset. This first lifeboat was small by modern standards, 36ft. by 8ft. 2ins., and was a pulling and sailing boat with 12 oars. She remained at Selsey for just four years and was only launched on two occasions, saving seven lives. The other permanent lifeboats to have been stationed at Selsey are *Four Sisters* (1871-85), *John and Henry Skynner* (1885-96), *Lucy Newbon* (1894-1919), *Jane Holland* (1922-29), *Canadian Pacific* (1929-37), *The Brothers* (1937-38), *Canadian Pacific II* (1938-69), *Charles Henry* (1969-83) and *City of London* (1983 to the present). Some of these lifeboats have been responsible for saving many lives. *Four Sisters*, for example, was launched 16 times and saved 49 lives, while *Canadian Pacific II*, which served during the Second World War, went out on 286 occasions and saved 157 lives.

Many different types of vessel are helped by the lifeboats. In August 1908 the *Lucy Newbon* rescued 63 people from the storm-tossed paddle steamer *Queen* after they had been stranded for a day and a night. The *Queen* ran day trips from Southampton to Brighton and got into difficulties off the Selsey coast owing to the breakdown of her steering gear during gales and torrential rain. The coxswain, Thomas Sparshott, praised the bravery of his crew, mentioning in particular 'one of our men, Arnell', who 'took off his lifebelt to get out of his oilskin so that he could wrap it round a woman'. In 1930, by contrast, the *Canadian Pacific* went out to a yacht, the *Lucy B* of Rye, which was in trouble to the west of Selsey Bill. Her anchor was not holding in the heavy seas and gale-force winds and the yacht was slowly being driven ashore. The anchor cable finally broke and, as the lifeboat arrived, the two men on board were about to make a desperate attempt to swim to the shore, a quarter of a mile away. For his gallant services in rescuing these men in appalling conditions and in only 6ft. of churning water, coxswain Frederick Barnes was awarded the R.N.L.I.'s bronze medal. Not all lifeboat stories have happy endings. In 1899 the *Arno*, a steamship with a crew of 17 on its way from Sunderland to Portsmouth with a cargo of coal, got into desperate trouble about eight miles south of Selsey Bill. The Selsey lifeboat was launched but, in the darkness and hampered by wind and huge waves, could not find the ship and returned empty handed. Eventually the crew abandoned ship but their small boat could not cope with the atrocious weather and most of the men were drowned. Six bodies were washed up on the shore at Bracklesham Bay and the *Arno* sank about four-and-a-half miles from Chichester Harbour.

In the early years, the Selsey lifeboats were launched over skids laid across the beach in front of the boathouse in 1866, but in May 1914 *The Chichester Observer* reported the completion of a wooden lifeboat slipway on the beach to the west of the boathouse. A large number of people assembled to watch the *Lucy Newbon* glide down this slipway for the first time. It was built on a pronounced slope, almost 15 ft. high at the top, and it took under 12 seconds

36. The crew of the Selsey lifeboat in their oilskins after rescuing passengers from the *Queen* on the night of 31 August/1 September 1908.

37. The launch of the *Lucy Newbon* on the new wooden slipway, 1914.

38. The crew of the Selsey lifeboat in 1904, with Coxswain Barnes standing on the right.

LIFE-BOAT

from the time the lifeboat was slipped till she touched the waves. Later, a new concrete slipway was built with a trolley and rails system to launch the boat smoothly. Sadly, the *Lucy Newbon* broke her back in 1919 while putting out to sea and was replaced in 1921 by the *Jane Holland*, Selsey's first self-righting motor lifeboat. She was capable of speeds of 7½ knots and could carry 60 men without sinking. Selsey and Bembridge had been selected to have new motor lifeboats as they were the stations from which the busy Solent shipping lane could best be protected.

In the 1920s coastal erosion seemed to worsen, perhaps due to the alteration in the tidal stream caused by the placing of a large number of concrete blocks at Spithead during the First World War. The lifeboat house, once well back on the beach, was now in danger of being undermined. The concrete slipway offshore was still intact and so it was decided to build a new boathouse out over the approach gangway. This was completed in 1927. However, by 1958 the boathouse which had been built only a few yards offshore was nearly 800 ft. out to sea and the gangway had to be extended every year. By 1958 the beach at Selsey had stabilised because of the new sea defences, so it was decided to build a new boathouse and slipway nearer the shore. A steel approach gangway, a boathouse and a reinforced concrete slipway were all built, and the new station was opened in 1960 by the Duke of Richmond and Gordon. Selsey's very first boathouse had cost £194 7s. to build, but the 1960 construction cost £75,000. A new boathouse for the inshore lifeboat was opened in May 1987. It has a storeroom and crewroom with hot water and a place to dry equipment. The old wooden boathouse has been renovated and re-sited to house a Selsey Lifeboat Museum.

The number of calls answered by the Selsey lifeboat increased steadily each year and so in March 1968 the R.N.L.I. allocated one of its new high-speed inflatable inshore lifeboats to the station. These need a crew of two or three men and are ideal for dealing with calls involving small yachts, dinghies and bathers, where speed is essential. In her first season the Selsey inshore boat was called out 16 times and helped nine boats.

In the past the crew of the Selsey lifeboat was made up completely of fishermen. In 1978 Mike Grant gave up his own fishing career and was appointed full-time coxswain. The only other full-time lifeboatman is Terry Wood, the mechanic. The rest of the crew, including a fireman, a policeman and a professional diver as well as many fishermen, are volunteers, called to a launch by bleepers in the case of boat officers or by a maroon. In earlier days one maroon meant stand to, two maroons meant a launch and three meant that a doctor was needed. Today there is a total crew list of 28, including two doctors (station medical advisers). Six men are needed to make up a crew on the present boat and there are always more volunteers than can be used. There is no shortage of young people wanting to join the service. They are trained on the inshore boat and all crew members receive training in first aid and the use of radar and other navigational aids. Service on the lifeboats often runs in families, sons following in their father's and grandfather's footsteps. There has been a Lawrence on the lifeboat crew, for example, from 1861 right up to the present. The first coxswain was James Lawrence, known as 'Pilot' Lawrence, who in 1886 was awarded a silver medal by the Life Boat Institution for his 'good and faithful service' – he was retiring after 25 years as coxswain. Today Len Lawrence is the longest serving member of the R.N.L.I. nationwide. He was a crewman from the age of 18, coxswain in 1961, and after retiring from active service became winchman. Even now, well over 80 years of age, he is boathouse keeper, and his son is a crew member. In 1968 Len was awarded a special R.N.L.I. long service badge for his work with the Selsey lifeboats.

In 1983 the Selsey station received the first of the new high-speed Tyne Class lifeboats. She cost £430,000 to build and was christened *City of London* because the money for her construction had been raised by a City of London special appeal. She is a self-righting,

39. The *City of London*, Selsey's current lifeboat, and the small inflatable inshore lifeboat alongside, in 1986.

steel-hulled boat, 47 ft. long and capable of a speed of 18 knots. She is fitted with radios, radar, automatic direction finding units and echo sounders, and carries first aid equipment, blankets, emergency rations and rescue gear. This boat can be in the water within six to ten minutes, day or night, after the decision is made to launch her. That decision rests with the Station Honorary Secretary, at present Mr. Clive Cockayne, who receives the request for help usually from H.M. Coastguard.

In the 125 years since the Selsey lifeboat station was established its offshore boats have been launched 654 times and saved 392 lives (figures for 1986), while the inflatable inshore boats have been called out 250 times since their introduction in 1968 and saved a further 88 lives – a record of which everyone in the village should be very proud. Selsey has come a long way from its early lifeboats which would have been launched by horses, and which relied on muscle power if there was no wind. But the same courage, resource and prompt action are still needed by today's crew as were shown by the crews back in the 19th century.

The Owers Light Vessel

Selsey lifeboatmen always took a cargo of Christmas fare to the captain and crew of the Owers lightship. The name Owers is a corruption of *Les Ours*, 'the bears', the name given by French sailors to the rocks which the lightship guarded, owing to their peculiar shape and formation.[22] Admiralty charts actually name an extensive series of banks running roughly from the old Medmerry Farm south-eastwards – Malt Owers, Middle Owers and

Outer Owers. The first light vessel was stationed near the Owers in 1788 by Trinity House, though poor holding ground meant that it was frequently dragged off station. In July 1882 a Captain Brooke reported to the Admiralty authorities that his vessel, Troopship *Assistance*, had touched the ground 7½ minutes after passing the Owers Light. A survey of the area was made in case a sandbank was developing, but in fact the lightship had just shifted a short distance towards the shore. On one occasion it drifted as far as St Valèry-en-Caux in France! The light vessel was an invaluable aid to sailors as a vast area of rocks and shoals extends up to seven miles south of Selsey Bill, making navigation hazardous and the erection of a fixed lighthouse impossible.

40. The Owers lightvessel, stationed far out to sea beyond the Owers rocks.

Between 1939 and 1973 the lightship most frequently used for the Owers was no. 3 light vessel. The hull of the lightship was red and on its side the name of the station was painted in huge white letters. It was 117 ft. long and provided accommodation for seven crewmen. There was a radio room, two 16-ft. lifeboats and of course the great light tower. During the 20th century the main light source was gradually changed from oil lamps to electric bulbs powered by diesel generators. Life on board the light vessel would have been monotonous, men keeping watch, eating their meals and sleeping in bunks below deck. On watch there would have been the rounds of the generators and air compressors, the logging of weather conditions, routine maintenance and lookout duties. The lightsmen did a month of duty before being brought ashore by tender or helicopter for a fortnight's relief work. In 1973 the light vessel was replaced by a large automatic navigation buoy (lanby) which gives a light comparable to the former light vessel. The lanby has a central pillar lantern standing some 15 metres above sea level and a circular deck beneath which are sealed compartments housing diesel generators. A telemetric link from St Catherine's lighthouse off the Isle of Wight monitors and controls the Owers buoy.

Selsey Coastguard Service

The lifeboat and coastguard services naturally work very closely together. The history of the coastguard service in Britain goes back much earlier than one might expect. At the end of the 13th century a system of coastguards was established for the defence of the country against the French, then in alliance with the Scots. William Dawtrey was appointed warden of West Sussex, with one mounted officer for each rape. In Selsey there were also four unmounted men to act as coastguards.

There have been many coastguard stations at Selsey over the years. Before a national coastguard service was founded in 1822 there was a Preventative Station in Fish Shop Lane in Selsey, and from 1809 members of the Preventative Water Guard were stationed there. In fact the census of 1851 still mentions a Henry Chesshyre serving at this station. The number of coastguards stationed in the village in the past is surprisingly large. The 1841 census lists 19 resident coastguards in the various stations. Coastguard stations obviously need to be built close to the shore and those in Selsey have therefore fallen victim to coastal erosion and been washed away by the sea.

The 'old' Thorney station, on the shores of Bracklesham Bay, was vacated in 1863 when high tides and gales broke down the shingle bank protecting it. It was replaced by Danner station which was in West Street like the present station – West Street was once called Danner Lane, from a field in the area said to have taken its name from the Danish invasion. This building was washed away in 1892 and replaced by another Thorney station. Thorney Drive was so named because it led to this station. There was also a coastguard look-out at Bill House,[23] on the tip of Selsey Bill, from a fairly early date. In the more recent past, there was a coastguard look-out at the old *Marine Hotel* from 1940 to 1945, which was burnt down. The present tower was constructed in 1972. There are mid-19th-century coastguard cottages behind this tower, but they are now privately owned. These are unusual for Sussex, the front face and the roof both hung with slates. The number of coastguard stations, some contemporaneous, is made clear by an entry in *Kelly's Directory* in 1899. This names Arthur McGill as chief coastguard officer at Selsey, on the site of the present lifeboat shed on the pier east of the Bill and washed away in about 1911; James Hembroke as chief boatman in charge at Thorney, with nine men; and George Thomson as chief boatman at the Wallend observation station (now a private house near Grange Farm), with nine men. However, by 1927 there is no mention of several stations and Ernest Haynes alone is named as station officer, with three men serving under him. Mr. Haynes, who continued to live locally after his retirement, did not die until the 1970s, at the age of 101 years. The earliest known coastguards serving in Selsey were Lieutenant James Thomas Nicholls, R.N., appointed Chief Officer of the Thorney station in 1831, and Lieutenant Thomas Heales, R.N., appointed Chief Officer of the Selsey Bill station in 1842.

During the First World War the service was under the control of the Admiralty and when the coastguards were called up for active service the boy scouts took over the Selsey and Thorney stations. They were visited by Sir Robert Baden-Powell in January 1915 and praised for their excellent work in ensuring the safety of the waters around the Selsey peninsula. In 1923 responsibility for the service passed to the Board of Trade and the coastguards officially took on their present day life-saving role. During the Second World War all emergency calls for Selsey came through the Royal Navy at Portsmouth and most rescues in those years involved aircraft. When the Admiralty had charge of the coastguard service the White Ensign was flown at stations but when the Board of Trade took over the

41. Early (pre-1907) view of the Thorney coastguard watch tower.

42. Coastguard signalling (semaphore) equipment on East Beach, *c.*1910. The lifeboat slipway can just be seen on the left of the picture – on dry land at this time!

43. Bill House, *c.*1955.

Union flag was used. In October 1974 a new coastguard ensign was flown for the first time and the local Methodist minister performed the change-over ceremony, hoisting the new flag on the top of the tower at Selsey.

Today H.M. Coastguard at Selsey is responsible for the sea from Pagham Harbour to Emsworth. There is excellent visibility from the tower – on a clear day one can see round the Isle of Wight to Fawley power station in the west and past Shoreham in the east. Until about 1985 the tower was under the control of a station officer, but now it is run purely by auxiliaries, 10 men led by Mr. Vic Littleboy, Auxiliary-in-Charge. The tower is manned 24 hours each day, through a standby watch; the men can be reached by telephone or pagers if a 999 call comes in, via Lee-on-Solent, the regional headquarters. Between 4 April and 4 October each year the tower is physically manned, as well as during Bank Holidays and casualty risk watches (bad weather), since more emergencies at sea are expected during all those times. The tower is also manned if the lifeboat is out on active service.

44. The Admiralty tower in 1987. Note the building in the background: how little it has changed since the start of the century (*see* no. 41).

H.M. Coastguards are sometimes involved in rescue work themselves, for example in beach searches or if the breeches buoy equipment is needed. Their main role, however, is to co-ordinate all sea rescue work, notifying the Honorary Secretary if the lifeboat is needed, calling in the police if a child is missing on the shore, or the search and rescue helicopter at Lee-on-Solent if that is required. Wessex helicopters are frequently used, especially in cases where people have been injured or are in the water and speed is essential. This has relieved some of the pressure on the lifeboat service. The coastguards deal with a great variety of calls, including bathers and surf boarders in difficulties, children drifting out to sea on dinghies, the exposure of suspicious objects on the beach, red flare distress signals from boats with engine failure, yachts which have gone aground, and ditched aircraft. The variety of vessels needing assistance from the coastguard service is revealed in the coastguard logbooks. A typical page covering 1950 mentions an aircraft down in the sea half a mile east of Thorney Island ('No hope of Pilot'); a small canoe capsized off Bognor rocks ('Two occupants picked up by Motor Boat'); a fishing boat capsized off Selsey Bill ('Two men overboard, one picked up by lifeboat, other helped ashore by lifelines' – the action taken by the Selsey men on this occasion was commended by H.M. Coastguard Inspector); a yacht, *Lady Jane*, drifting at sea ('lifeboat took her in tow and brought her to moorings at Selsey').

The coastguard tower has sophisticated direction-finding equipment which enables the auxiliaries to locate boats in distress and pick up men's voices over a special V.H.F. radio channel. This is all a far cry from the original coastguard service established in 1822 to crack down on smuggling and save lives if ships were wrecked. The station at Selsey is always busy – in 1986, for example, 76 emergency calls were received.

The Fire Service

In December 1909 a fire occurred at Hilton's Farm in Selsey. At that time the village had no fire brigade of its own so, by the time the Chichester brigade arrived, the fire had a good hold on the farm buildings in spite of the attempts made by local men to extinguish the flames with buckets of water. The fire was prevented from spreading to adjoining cottages, but corn sheds, stables and bathing machines stored in the vicinity were all badly burned, resulting in £400 worth of damage. The damage would have been far greater if it had not been for the plentiful supply of water from Selsey's newly-opened waterworks (*see* page 70). Only a few weeks after this fire, the villagers decided that a volunteer fire brigade should be formed so that Selsey would not be dependent on firemen stationed eight miles away. The parish council agreed to spend £42 15s. 6d. on the necessary equipment, including a hose cart and lamps. Helmets and belts were bought for the men, as well as 500 ft. of hose and a portable hand pump. Mr. E. G. Arnell offered to store the plant free of charge and it was decided to ask Mr. A. J. Cutler, ex-captain of the Chichester fire brigade, to be in charge of Selsey's newly-formed service.

Sadly, this early fire brigade gradually broke up and by the 1920s Selsey's police constable, A. J. Pope, was helping to extinguish fires with other volunteers. In 1925 one of the oldest buildings in Selsey High Street, a picturesque thatched cottage adjoining the Methodist church, was completely destroyed by fire. Mr. Lewis Maidment from the local garage brought his stock of fire extinguishers and a number of volunteers were soon on the scene. The Chichester fire brigade arrived after almost an hour, by which time the flames had gained a firm hold. Swiss Cottage was the property of the Methodists and had been occupied for 34 years by Mr. Willshire, caretaker of the chapel. The cottage was at least 200 years old. Immediately after this disaster the parish council spent considerable time discussing the possibility of re-forming the official fire brigade. The original appliances had been stored at Maidment's Garage and would only need minor repairs to become operative again.

After years of wrangling, the Selsey fire brigade was revived in January 1927. It consisted of Captain W. E. Mitchell, Lieutenant R. Selsby, Deputy Officer G. Williams, and eight firemen. They were to be paid for attending fires and this money was claimed back from insurance companies. For the first hour officers were paid 5s. and firemen 4s., and they would receive 2s. 6d. per hour after that. It was decided to erect an electric 'klaxon' on Mr. Maidment's premises in the High Street to summon the brigade in case of fire. Helmets and 150 ft. of new hose had been purchased by March 1925. By the 1930s the Captain of Selsey fire brigade was Ralph Selsby, a coal merchant by trade, and he was complaining of antiquated fire-fighting appliances, the shortage of fire hydrants in many new roads, and the lack of a motor fire engine. Also there was insufficient hose to reach from one hydrant to another and the pressure was too low to produce a powerful jet of water. Modern equipment was essential because the nearest brigade was eight miles away in Chichester.

This was all made painfully obvious in May 1932 when the Selsey brigade was called to a fire in a council house in Beach Road. The men arrived quickly, located the fire in a back bedroom and Captain Selsby organised a 'bucket party' of neighbours and sent for the fire extinguisher. A search was made for the nearest fire hydrant and this was found in Manor Road, buried in the grass. The hose was fixed to it and then found to be 40 ft. too short. By this time the fire had been brought under control by a fire extinguisher borrowed

45. Ralph Selsby stands proudly in front of Selsey's fire engine in the 1930s.

from Mr. Maidment rather than belonging to the brigade! If the wind had been stronger that day, the inadequate equipment could have led to disaster. A ratepayers' meeting was held in the church hall the following month to discuss the situation. Mr. W. F. Hopkins, Chairman of the Fire Brigade Committee, moved that Selsey have a motor fire engine to replace the 'utterly useless fire appliances at present in stock'.[24] It took the Chichester brigade 35 minutes to get to Selsey, during which time a thatched cottage could easily be burnt to the ground if the wind was strong. A resolution to purchase an engine at a cost not exceeding £1,000 was passed almost unanimously. In July 1932 two demonstrations were given by Ford and Morris engines. Large crowds gathered to watch the displays but finally a Dennis fire engine was bought the following year. It was almost unheard of for such a small community to possess its own motor engine in those days, but Selsey's isolated location had made the purchase imperative. Some amusing incidents were recorded in the early years. In November 1934, for example, the brigade was called to a rick fire at Fish Shops Farm. Such was the speed at which the crew turned out that two arrived without their false teeth – a problem when it came to eating their bread and cheese afterwards!

Selsey's fire brigade, like those up and down the country, was kept very busy during the Second World War. On 13 August 1940 the A.R.P. recorded: 'German plane crashed in field past Medmerry. All Germans were burnt in plane. Selsey Fire Brigade in action'. On the night of 9 April 1941 between 200 and 300 incendiaries were dropped on and around Broadreeds. The dining hall caught alight and the fire brigade was at work there for many hours. The National Fire Service was founded in 1940 and took over responsibility for the Selsey fire brigade which had been maintained by the parish council since its inauguration in 1910.

Today Selsey has a fire station in the High Street which is manned by a voluntary crew, backed up by a full-time service operating from Chichester. Tony Dann is Station Officer.

The Police

Before the First World War there was a single policeman for the village, living in rented accommodation in Station Road (now Church Road). The first police constable recorded in Selsey was George Benford, mentioned in the 1871 census returns as living 'in the village' with his wife and three children. By 1881 his name was replaced by that of Stephen Bond, born in London. In 1899 Henry Beacher was Selsey's constable, representing the county police force, the West Sussex Constabulary, which had been founded in 1857. In 1925 P.C. Pope, who had been at Selsey for over 12 years and was a valued member of the community, was transferred to Felpham. He had first come to Selsey from Chichester to deal with break-ins at unoccupied houses during the winter, mostly Londoners' summer residences. In 1927 *Kelly's Directory* speaks of a Police Station, with two constables, W. H. J. Osman and C. G. Morris. Both or one of these men must have lived in Mrs. E. Burchell's house, Milford Cottage, as the 1926 Rate Book names the West Sussex Police Force as occupying the property. In the 1930s there were complaints about inadequate policing in the village. Even though it had now become a popular seaside resort there was still only one resident constable, Mr. Osman. Just prior to the Second World War the old police cottages were built and the new Police Station in Chichester Road was completed in about 1970.

Water, Sewage and Drainage, and Refuse

Until the first decade of this century Selsey's needs were supplied by spring water. Early maps of the peninsula show wells following the line of the few made-up roads and cart tracks because there was no piped water supply. In December 1906 a Bill was proposed in Parliament which would give Selsey and seven neighbouring parishes an independent water supply from the Chichester reservoir. The Selsey Water Act was finally passed in July 1907, under the terms of which the Chichester corporation was to supply 'pure and wholesome water' at 6d. per 1,000 gallons. The Selsey Waterworks were officially opened by the Mayor of Chichester on 19 December 1908. There would be a minimum daily supply of 100,000 gallons, which would help Selsey's growth both as a residential area and as a holiday resort. The water tower was in School Lane. During the 1920s there was a great outcry in the village when the water rates were increased, partly because of the rise in demand for water because of the many new housing estates being built at that time. In August 1929 there was a water shortage due to lack of rain and the Water Company forbade the use of water for gardening, washing cars or horses, or washing down yards and outbuildings. In the 1950s, when its resident population was just over 4,000, the village was still supplied with water by the Selsey Water Company, but today the Portsmouth Water Company has taken over that role. In 1983 the Selsey scouts launched an appeal to raise money to pay for the demolition of the 60 ft. high water tower, which was threatening the safety of their premises in School Lane. It was finally pulled down in June 1984.

Selsey has always been a very difficult place to drain economically, as there is subsoil water only a few feet below the surface of the ground. In 1901 *The West Sussex Gazette* carried an article entitled 'Selsey's Sanitary Sore', which explained that Westhampnett Rural Council had recently reported that Selsey should have a proper sewerage scheme. At that

46. Cartoon about 'Ye Selsea Water Supplie' from *The Chichester Observer*, December 1908.

time all sewage from the cess pits and pools honeycombing the village left by a drain which had been laid from the High Street by the side of East Road. This was a surface water drain, constructed from clay pipes and laid without joints. For most of its length the drain was now choked up and utterly useless. After even a moderate fall of rain (half an inch in 24 hours) the sewage welled up into a ditch by the side of the road. Earlier in 1901 sewage and surface water extended right across Selsey's roads – this naturally caused considerable public alarm at a time when diphtheria and typhoid epidemics were frequent. A proper sewerage system, at an estimated cost of £2,500, was recommended.

In 1902 Mr. W. L. Barrett, formerly town surveyor for Bognor, was appointed to prepare plans for a drainage scheme. He proposed a single sewer outfall at Selsey Bill, to be under water at all states of the tide. There would be a 4 ft. barrel sewer to hold all sewage from the district at low tide when it could not be discharged into the sea. A series of 18- and 9-inch pipes would gravitate to this tank, which could be emptied twice every 24 hours. Flushing would have to be done by means of water carts and wells until the urgently-required public water supply was installed. Unfortunately, experiments with floats proved that any sewage discharged into the sea in this way would flow east and would ruin both the fishing industry and Selsey's reputation for clean beaches. Mr. Barrett's plan was therefore abandoned.

It was not until 1914 that a sewerage and drainage scheme was finally agreed upon at a meeting of Westhampnett R.D.C. The plan was to keep most of the sewage tanks beyond Crablands Farm, but it was recognised that crude sewage could not be discharged into the sea because of the peculiar currents around the Bill which would wash it ashore again. In any case, it would ruin the fishing industry as prawns, lobsters and crabs in particular suffer when brought into contact with any form of sewage. About six miles of sewers would be required at an average depth of 8 ft. and these would deal with household sewage only, not rainwater and road drainage. The pipes would be capable of handling sewage from over 4,000 people, the winter population of Selsey at the start of the century being about 1,500. This was to allow for expansion of the permanent population and for visitors in the summer. The cost was estimated at £12,500, necessitating an extra rate of 2s. or more. This would make house rents very expensive and it was feared that people would not choose to live in the village. However, visitors in the past had been critical of the primitive sanitary arrangements in Selsey – previously sewage had been ploughed into the land – and reports of medical officers had long stated that a proper system of sewage disposal was essential. The plan was therefore put into operation.

By the early 1930s it was becoming obvious that even this system was inadequate and that Selsey needed mains drainage. The population of the village had doubled since 1914 and, by 1931, 200 houses were connected to one sewer built after the First World War in Manor Road and Station Road for 40-50 houses. Other houses in the village, including all those being newly built, relied on cesspools. It was estimated that a scheme for the proper drainage of Selsey would cost about £50,000. The majority of ratepayers agreed that the inevitable increase in rates would be justified to prevent some sewage filtering into the subsoil and the rest being discharged on to the foreshore as was happening at that time. Dr. Barford spoke in favour of mains drainage on health grounds. In March 1934 the parish council decided that all streets should be given mains drainage at public expense, regardless of whether or not they were private roads.

The lack of a proper sewerage system was not the only threat to the health of Selsey's residents at the start of the present century. In 1911 there were reports of a ditch in the village, adjoining the Parsonage Croft footpath, being used as a refuse tip. Eventually an arrangement was reached with a local contractor and the refuse was removed to the level of the top of the ditch and it was then covered with ash and gravel. The year 1928 witnessed the start of a service to collect and dispose of household waste in Selsey. Westhampnett R.D.C. signed a contract with Messrs. R. Selsby & Co. of the High Street, who were to collect refuse for the next three years. The Council agreed to provide every house with a proper receptacle in which to store ashes and refuse.

Electricity and Gas

In the early 1920s there was great controversy, reported at length in the local newspapers, concerning a proposal to install gas or electric lamps in Selsey's streets. The fishermen, most of whom would have gone to bed early anyway, opposed the idea of any form of street lighting (as they had ever since the issue was first raised in 1900), feeling that it would damage Selsey's rural charm and fearing higher rates (4s. 6d. in the pound in 1924). However, they were outvoted at a general meeting of residents in 1924 and in November of that year electricity first reached Selsey from Chichester, an underground supply costing about £25,000. In November 1925 Selsey residents voted overwhelmingly in favour of electric rather than gas lamps and agreed that Chichester corporation should supply 30 electric lamps for the village streets to be lit from dusk to midnight at a cost of £4 4s. per lamp each year. During the course of the next year most shops had electric lighting installed and many private houses, too. By April 1926 all the principal streets, including Station Road, New Road, Manor Road, Grafton Road and Seal Road, were lit by electric lamps

Street Lighting

OF

SELSEY.

A PARISH MEETING

WILL BE HELD ON

FRIDAY, FEB. 1st, 1924, at 7.30 p.m.

IN THE

COUNCIL INFANTS' SCHOOL,

To discuss the question of Public Lighting and to adopt the "Lighting and Watching Act, 1833," if the Meeting so decides.

If you want your Streets Light and Safe you must attend this Meeting and VOTE for it.

Only Ratepayers are allowed to VOTE, and a two-thirds majority is necessary to carry the Scheme.

It is proposed to provide about 18 GAS LAMPS, and the cost will involve a 2d. Rate—less than 2/- per Lamp per week.

Outlying parts of the Parish, as Church Norton, East Beach, etc., will not be included and the Ratepayers in such Districts will not be asked to contribute.

If you want LIGHT this is your opportunity to secure it.

L. H. TURTLE, "Croindene," Selsey.

47. Street lighting notice, 1924.

and East Street, Clayton Road and High Street soon followed suit.

There had long been gasworks in Selsey, in Warner's Lane. Luther Clayton and his brother had founded the Selsey Gas and Coke Company in about 1880 and in April 1901 the Petersfield and Selsey Gas Bill (a private measure) passed the committee stage in the House of Commons. Most people in the village had gas lighting in their homes until the mid-1920s when electricity was more widely available. In the early days, large boats brought coal to the beach for the gasworks (*see* page 129). As we have seen, the works were badly flooded in 1910 and a similar calamity occurred in November 1931. In 1930 the Petersfield and Selsey Gas Company had offices on the east side of the High Street. These, and the Selsey Water Company offices next door, were managed by Walter Clement Rose. The gasworks finally ceased operating around 1956. Most of the buildings were dismantled and those remaining quickly fell into ruin.

Health Services

In view of Selsey's poor sanitary conditions prior to the start of the present century, it is perhaps not surprising that there were periodic outbreaks of disease. An epidemic raged in the village between July and October 1854, for example. A Mr. James Sotcher wrote to his grandson in South Australia early in 1855, reporting that he 'was just recovering from a severe fit of sickness. We had 27 people died in Selsea in 3 months'. The cause of the epidemic is unknown but its severity can be gauged by the fact that 16 people were buried in the parish in September 1854 alone. Later, in January 1911, the Local Government Board received a letter mentioning an alleged epidemic of diphtheria in Selsey. By 1913 diphtheria in the village had been reported in such a way that outsiders compared it with the great plague of the 17th century, though in fact there had been only 25 to 30 cases.

Evidence for early medical care for the villagers is sketchy. The 1841 census lists Lucy Woodland, aged 65, as a nurse and the 1851 census describes Sheila Lambeth and Charlotte Harp as nurses. Later censuses in the 19th century make no mention of either nurses or doctors and in 1875, when a nine-year-old boy was badly injured by a horse, *The West Sussex Gazette* reported that he was taken to Mr. Cresswell, a surgeon in Sidlesham, indicating that at that time Selsey had no doctor of its own. One of the village's earliest doctors was James Edward Felix André, a physician and surgeon in Sidlesham from the 1890s who later opened a surgery in Selsey High Street. By 1918 he had formed a joint practice with Dr. Arthur Armitage Humphrys. At the same time Miss Agnes Olive Blacklocks of East Street was district nurse. Selsey's first dentist seems to have been Bernard Westlake, in practice in East Street in 1909. By 1927 he had been replaced by John Gillman, who attended surgery between 10 a.m. and 6 p.m. on Tuesdays and Saturdays. By 1915 the Selsey church school log-book (*see* page 77) was reporting annual medical examinations on the eight- and 12-year-old children, and periodic visits by individual children to the school clinic for dental treatment. The welfare of children had been one of the priorities of the Liberal governments of 1906-14. On 16 May 1930 the headmaster of the school reported, 'The Milk Club commenced on Monday morning with 21 children but today it numbers 31. The milk is supplied from the local dairy in bottles holding one third of a pint'. Sadly, this did not prevent entries like that made in November 1934, 'Dr. Smedley called and examined the children and picked out cases of malnutrition'.

In 1973 a Health Centre was opened by West Sussex County Council in St Peter's Crescent which now provides consulting rooms and offices for six general practitioners as well as nursing and clerical staff. An answering service advises callers how to contact the duty doctor outside the Centre's normal hours. Two of the Health Centre's practitioners, Dr. Andrew Murphy and Dr. Edwin Wrigley, were awarded silver statuettes by the R.N.L.I. in April 1987, in recognition of their devoted work with the lifeboat service in Selsey.

built to cater for 210 children and at the turn of the century average attendance was 120 juniors and 50 infants. Year after year school inspectors gave glowing reports of the school and its headteacher. In 1879 the diocesan inspector stated: 'The results of the examination were again a credit to Miss Morris. The tone of the school, the discipline and the intelligence make it a pleasure to work in it. I have no hesitation in saying that this school is a model one.'

In 1902 Balfour passed an Act which gave the elected county councils the power to provide for education in their area. Local authorities were now to maintain all elementary schools, including those founded by religious bodies, as Selsey's had been. Until this time no rate had been levied for maintaining the village school, the parish magazine reminding parishioners 'that they have only escaped the duty of paying such a rate by the charity of a few (a very few) voluntary subscribers'. In fact, the Rector of Selsey had practically assumed financial responsibility for the school himself, but this meant that there were insufficient funds to provide up-to-date equipment or certificated teachers. The new Education Act meant that the school premises continued to be owned by the Rector and churchwardens and could be used by them for Sunday School and other parochial purposes. The appointment of teachers was to remain in their hands, though subject to confirmation by the local authority. Nonconformists could now become assistant teachers for the first time. The local authority, however, would be responsible for the payment of all teachers and for the provision of equipment. Costs would be met from the usual government grant, supplemented by an education rate, probably 4d. in the pound to begin with, levied by the county council. Selsey residents were asked to continue to make voluntary subscriptions to pay for improvements to the premises; otherwise new buildings would be provided by the local education authority and rates would be raised considerably to meet the cost.

By 1903 the old premises were overcrowded and insanitary and the County Council Education Committee ordered the Managers to provide new accommodation for the village's schoolchildren. A new infants' school was built at the corner of the High Street and Cross Road (now School Lane), three-quarters of the cost paid for out of the rates. The total cost, including furniture, amounted to £1,691 and the school opened in June 1905. It was built to accommodate 110 children but by 1909 average attendance was only 53. Miss Annie Reynolds was headmistress of the infants' school from the time it opened until well into the 1920s. The original building is now part of Medmerry County Primary School, recognisable in the ground plan and elevation prepared by the architects. By then demands were being made for better facilities at the old mixed voluntary school in the High Street. The Board of Education insisted that new offices and two new cloakrooms should be built, otherwise new council schools would be erected at a cost of £3,000 which would be charged to Selsey parish. The Rector therefore made a superhuman effort to raise £100 through subscriptions to improve the church school which was excellent in other respects, and avoid the extra burden on parochial rates.

Samuel Dewey, who lived at 'Oakwood' in New Road, was headmaster of Selsey's 'big' school (for juniors) from 1894, retiring in 1931. The log-book kept at the mixed national school between 1906 and 1937 is still extant.[26] This describes the school as having a main room, 34 ft. by 17 ft., a second room 27 ft. by 16 ft., and a third room 17 ft. by 14 ft. In 1906 the staff consisted of Samuel Dewey as headmaster, 'certificated and trained', who had charge of standards VI and VII (the oldest children), Emma Elizabeth Archer, a 'certificated assistant' in charge of standards IV and V, Elizabeth Sedgley Buchan, an 'uncertificated assistant' in charge of standards I and II, and Harriet Fanny Goodger, a 'supplementary' who looked after the standard III children. Mrs. Dewey later joined the teaching staff of the school. Some idea of the lessons available to the pupils other than the three Rs is given in a list at the front of the log-book. Needlework was taught to the girls by Miss Archer

50. Selsey schoolchildren outside their classroom *c.*1910 with their headmistress, Miss Reynolds. The children are, from left to right: *top row*, Fred Jones, Bob Terry, Hilda Johnson, Florrie Wingham, ? , Edward Jupp, Sidney Winslade; *middle row*, Daisy Sherrington, Lucy Arnell, Elsie Lawrence, Vera Lawrence, Gertrude Lawrence, Ivy Harris, Dorothy Grigg, Bertha Male, Lily Lee; *front row*, Leslie Fullick, Walter Ransome, Edward Matthews, Percy Matthews, Reggie Giles and Alf Mant.

assisted by Miss Goodger, the boys were taught drawing by the headmaster assisted by Miss Buchan, cookery was taken by Miss Archer and swimming by the headmaster. In 1910 a school inspector complained that only boys were given drawing lessons, not the girls. It is hard to discover the rationale behind this discrimination. The school was regularly inspected and was always praised for its educational standards. The diocesan report in December 1906 stated: 'The teachers have done conscientious and painstaking work with excellent results. The children take much interest in their subjects and answered thoughtfully.' In the early years of the 20th century, the school leaving age was 14, Samuel Dewey recording in June 1914 'Herbert Smart said "goodbye" today, being 14 years of age on Saturday'. There was, however, what was popularly known as the 'Labourer Exam', taken by children who needed to leave school earlier than their 14th birthday in order to help their parents at work.

In 1906 there were 156 children on the school books and many entries in the log relate to attendance. The informality of the system deserves some comment. In the early years of the century headteachers had it in their power to close the school at will and Samuel Dewey was no exception. He closed Selsey school for the typical outbreaks of infectious diseases such as that of whooping cough which began with the Sherrington family in January 1907 and caused him to shut up shop for five weeks in March and April of that year. He also closed the school for the children to go blackberrying, to attend chapel Sunday School outings to Goodwood, and because of a boy scout parade in Chichester. On 4 July 1906 he recorded, 'The school was closed in the afternoon owing to a circus coming for the first time into the village and the children naturally wanting to attend the afternoon performance', and on 12 July 1923 the school was closed at 3.15 p.m. 'to enable those children who wished to do so to take part in the Sand Competition of the Daily Mail'. Many modern schoolchildren might long for such an understanding headteacher. Low attendance was recorded over the years due to colds and influenza, diphtheria, chickenpox, rainy weather, and the beginning of the summer season – in July 1907 Samuel Dewey reported, 'The attendance this week has fallen owing to the influx of visitors, parents wanting elder children to assist them'. One of the saddest causes of low attendance was, of course, war. On 7 September 1914, the first school day after the summer holidays, the entry in the log-book reads, 'Many are away, engaged as errand boys, some helping the father with the boat in place of men called up for war, and the Boy Scouts are being employed by the Admiralty'. By December 1914 eleven scouts were absent from the school.

The war had a considerable impact on the life of Selsey schoolchildren, even those who were not members of the scout movement. Many boys were given special permission by the L.E.A. to leave school at the earlier age of 13 in order to go out to work because of the shortage of men in the village. In September 1914 the headmaster recorded, 'The schoolhouse being in the occupation of soldiers on duty in Selsey, the Cookery class has not been held'. Other disruptions caused by the war included 'the experiment of blowing up bridges and buildings' in May 1915. The blowing up of an old barn at Medmerry caused several of the boys to be late for school that day. Samuel Dewey himself was obliged to undertake military duties with the Sussex Volunteer Force in spite of his continued employment at the school – on several occasions he records that he had to miss classes because he had been away the night previously on duty either at Littlehampton or guarding ammunition trains at Ford. Selsey's schoolchildren made their own contribution to the war effort. In December 1915 they sent one pound to the Overseas Club (which supplied Christmas gifts to soldiers and sailors), on 10 July 1916 the older pupils were allowed to leave school early to sell flags and collect 'on behalf of the Belgian children', and in June 1917 they began a collection of eggs for those wounded in the war.

The log-book supplies many other fascinating details about life in Selsey school in the first half of this century. It is surprising to find that boys were in some ways at more of a disadvantage than girls, especially as far as higher education was concerned. In August 1921 H.M.I. Mr. Russell reported that 'while girls who reach a sufficiently high standard have the opportunity of attending the Chichester Secondary School for Girls, no boys are able to receive a secondary education unless their parents can afford to send them to a boarding school. It is most desirable therefore that the general equipment of the school should be improved and that the standard reached by the brighter boys should not be limited by the dearth of suitable books'. He comments in particular on the shortage of geography books and atlases. There are several mentions of older girls having gained free places at the High School for Girls at Chichester. The vast majority of girls who left Selsey school at the age of 14, however, entered domestic service rather than continuing their education. Other official complaints about the school during this period concerned the small size and poor drainage of the school playground, the overcrowding of the classsrooms (in 1930 for example, Mr. Dewey was teaching 52 children in one classroom), and the poor sanitary conditions – in June 1932 the headmaster complained that the pails in the girls' closets were not being emptied daily by the caretaker. Conditions were worse in the winter when the school was not adequately heated. In December 1932 temperatures fell to 38°F in the classrooms because of a shortage of stoves. Those who remember Mr. Dewey describe him as a hard task-master in his later years, not averse to the use of corporal punishment to maintain discipline. For talking or misbehaving in class, boys were given six 'cuts' of his cane on each hand; four 'cuts' were meted out for being late to lessons, and two for poor effort. Detention after school was also used as a punishment for both boys and girls.

In February 1932 Mr. Neville Hammond was appointed to replace Mr. Dewey and introduced organised games for the first time – football, cricket and boxing, with stoolball for the girls. He acquired a piece of land next to the school playing fields and pupils were given small plots in which to grow flowers and vegetables of their choice. He recorded with great pride in July 1935, '80 lbs. new potatoes dug, 20 lbs. peas' – the first school harvest. Mr. Hammond widened the curriculum at Selsey school in many other ways: he introduced radio broadcasts, the teaching of folk dancing, experimental work in science lessons, and the production of dramatic performances (especially the Christmas pantomime) and a school magazine. In October 1936 he reported to the children the death of Samuel Dewey, headmaster of the school for 37 years. A service of remembrance was held in the church hall and wreaths were sent to the funeral from pupils and staff. The church school finally became a council school in about 1937 after which time a new log book was begun which has not yet come to light.

Attempts were also made to improve the education of Selsey's adult population. The Selsey Reading Room and Bungalow Club opened in October 1889, offering constructive occupation to villagers particularly during the winter months. After the club's first season, a supper was held at the Malt House and Mr. Lambert Stubington made a speech in which he claimed that such societies ranked among 'the most useful means of conveying knowledge and promoting happiness'. In 1908 the Selsey Institute was opened to supply both social and educational facilities. The hall, now the British Legion hall in the High Street, was built in 1885 and was capable of seating 250. It housed a billiard table, a small temperance refreshment bar, and a library with a nucleus of 250 volumes given by Peter Keary, the president. The hall could also be used for concerts and public meetings. On the opening night 101 members had already paid their subscriptions (a minimum of 2d. per week) to the Institute, which was non-political and non-sectarian. By 1909 many concerts had been held at the Institute and its library had expanded to 329 volumes. As early as 1938 the Misses M. and G. Soare organised a circulating library in the church hall (now the parish hall) in the High Street; today the public library has its own modern octagonal building in School Lane.

The East Street school, originally the Selsey Council Senior and Junior Mixed School, was erected in 1938 and was inspected by Queen Elizabeth, the Queen Mother, soon after it was opened. It was to provide education for children between the ages of eight and 14 years. Mr. C. H. E. Cox was headmaster from 1942 until his retirement in 1973. When he took over the school was, to quote the late Mr. Alan Kite, a school manager, 'at a very low ebb'; one of the classrooms was used as a potato store, the art room was used only once a week by the county library, and the new science equipment had never yet been used. The timetable made no mention of games and the volunteers who had run the school canteen had ceased to operate. Mr. Cox quickly made efforts to develop the school and improve standards. Soon children from other schools, in Sidlesham and Mundham, were coming to Selsey to use the woodwork and domestic science facilities. A strong sporting tradition was built up and children were encouraged to remain at school after reaching the official leaving age, learning typewriting and other skills to help them in later life.

The Institute had lapsed by the 1940s but Mr. Cox revived it in the form of a youth club/evening institute at the school, with activities including typewriting, shorthand, woodwork, drama, ballroom dancing, cricket, soccer and competitive boxing. In about 1946 the children of Selsey were first entered for external examinations, R.S.A. and Aircraft Apprentices. In the 1950s the Selsey schools were reorganised. The East Street school became the Selsey County Secondary Modern in September 1953, taking in all pupils of 11-plus age from Selsey and Sidlesham, and in the following year from the two schools in the Witterings also. The Selsey juniors were to travel to Sidlesham to school.

Later in the 1950s another reorganisation allowed Selsey's primary-aged children to be educated within the village itself and in 1962 Mr. Alan Eames became head of Selsey Primary School in School Lane. In 1965, however, coinciding with the opening of the first phase of the Manhood Secondary School, the Selsey juniors moved to the East Street premises as the School Lane buildings were needed to provide sufficient classroom accommodation for the older children until their purpose-built school on the other side of the road was complete. The old East Street secondary buildings were remodelled and converted, and all the appropriate facilities for teaching younger children were installed. Selsey Primary School was then officially re-opened in 1967 by County Councillor Brigadier Thwaites and renamed Seal County Primary School. This was followed by a boom in Selsey's population between 1967 and 1977 so that by 1972 the school, designed for only eight classes, had nearly 600 pupils between the ages of five and eleven on roll. Ten units of temporary accommodation had to be erected in the grounds to cope with all these children. To relieve the pressure on Seal School, Medmerry Primary School was opened in 1973 in the old School Lane premises which had by then been vacated by the Manhood School. Parents were given the option of taking their children from the Seal School to Medmerry. Alan Eames remained headmaster at Seal until his retirement in December 1986. Mr. Peter Guy was appointed as headmaster at Medmerry in 1973 and filled that role until July 1986.

As mentioned earlier, the Manhood Secondary School was opened in School Lane in January 1965, the foundation stone having been laid by the Duke of Norfolk in September 1963. It cost about £75,000 to build, which gives some idea of inflation since the infants' school had been built (for £1,691) at the start of the century. The Manhood School provided a balanced education for the peninsula's secondary schoolchildren, placing equal emphasis on the academic, practical and sporting aspects of the curriculum. Specialist rooms for woodwork, art, domestic science, metalwork, science, and commercial studies were available, and a swimming pool was built, the money being raised by staff, pupils and parents. During the late 1960s it was expected that the Manhood School would become comprehensive. However, the education authorities decided that it should become a Middle School and that Manhood children aged 13 and over should travel to a comprehensive school in Chichester. Teachers, parents and governors alike resisted and, in 1973 when Mr. Cox retired, Mr. Barnett was appointed headmaster of the Manhood Comprehensive School. To make the school a viable comprehensive, it was decided to include children of the 10-11 age group, giving Selsey's secondary school a unique age range of 10-16 years. Both primary schools therefore lost their oldest children. As a result of this, the division of Selsey's primary children between two schools, and the natural slowing down in development in the village which occurred at this time, the school populations were reduced to more manageable proportions. Seal School in the mid-1970s had about 240 on roll, the sort of number it was designed to house, and Medmerry educated about 180 children.

Today the East Street premises house Seal School which, along with Medmerry School, provides Selsey children with education from the age of five to ten years. Each school caters for around 200 children. The comprehensive school in School Lane is now known as Manhood Community College and has gained such a good reputation that people are moving into Selsey so that their children can be educated there. Its pupils are drawn mainly from Selsey and Sidlesham but also from the Witterings. Its academic results are good, as are its musical and sporting achievements. In July 1984, pupils in the Manhood School Showband were finalists in the All England Schools' Big Band section at the National Festival of Music for Youth held at the Queen Elizabeth Hall on the South Bank, London. The band has also broadcast on Radio Sussex and supports many local fund-raising activities. The new Manhood buildings include a purpose-built youth wing which has developed into an adult education centre under the leadership of Mr. Jonathan Craven, the youth tutor. So, as its new name suggests, the school is used for the benefit of the whole community.

* * * * *

There were private preparatory schools in Selsey from an early date and, even earlier, children from privileged families must have been educated at home – the 1861 census records Louisa Clayton of Glynn House working as a governess. There has always been a profusion of private schools in seaside resorts, as they could recommend the healthy climate, good air and safe bathing of their location. On 5 January 1865, Mrs. Fleetwood of Sparks House, Selsey, advertised her 'Young Ladies' Boarding School' in *The West Sussex Gazette* in this rather pompous way:

> A sound English education is imparted; with French and Music. Terms 20 guineas. Little boys under 10 years of age are received. Delicate children would find a home of comfort in this healthy and pleasant little town, so near the sea.

No further advertisement for this school appears in later editions of the newspaper, so it is not certain that Mrs. Fleetwood's establishment ever got off the ground. A little later, in 1886, a Mrs. Binstead is recorded as running a Ladies' School at Beacon House and in October 1919 Samuel Dewey recorded in the church school log-book, 'A new private school having been opened in the village, many of the tradespeople's children have left to attend it as being more select'. This was probably the Dame School recalled by several elderly residents of the village which was opened in Hillfield Road about that time by Miss Donkin and Miss Lack.

Some private schools were very short-lived, such as Miss Nellie Pearse's preparatory school which is mentioned in *Kelly's Directory* for 1909 but was in existence for only a few years. Others had a much longer life. In 1930 Mrs. E. B. Owen opened Gwendon Preparatory School at Broombank in Manor Road near the *Selsey Hotel*. The name was soon changed to Broombank Boarding School and as such it was still being advertised well into the 1950s. The two Misses Morgan later took over from Mrs. Owen. In Mrs. Owen's day, pupils of this select alternative to the Council school wore a blue blazer with a white 'G' on the pocket for 'Gwendon'; the uniform was later changed to a brown blazer with a red 'B' for 'Broombank'. Many children from outside Selsey attended this school: the carriers were kept busy at the start and end of each term, transporting trunks to and from Chichester station. The school was surrounded by extensive grounds and dancing displays were held in the open air in the summer.

There was a considerable growth in the number of private schools nationwide in the 1940s and 1950s due to the post-war 'baby boom'. Private preparatory schools in Selsey during this period included Datcha School in Coxes Road, a kindergarten run by a Miss

Davey, Halton House School in Manor Road and St Wilfrid's School in Hillfield Road. The latter was for day pupils only, both boys and girls, between the ages of four and fifteen. It was established around 1937 by Mrs. Nixey. She re-opened just after the war, by which time she had re-married and was Mrs. Durston. The 40 or so children attending school in her house wore a red and grey uniform. The house is now the *Seal Hotel.* Bourne House School was the only independent school in Selsey given official recognition as 'efficient' by the Ministry of Education. It was founded in 1959 and provided education for boys between the ages of three and seven, and girls between three and thirteen. The school, with Miss Webb as principal, was situated in Hillfield Road only 300 yards from the sea and prided itself on 'creating a happy atmosphere, children being treated as individuals, with emphasis on discipline, good manners and deportment, spiritual knowledge and physical well-being'. Most of these private schools had closed by the 1970s.

YOUR CHILD'S CAREER

Written Examination Successes
in 1952—1953

7 Secondary School Selection Examinations
8 Common Entrances to Public Schools
1 Public School Presentation
and the Highest Honour :
1 Public School Scholarship (Value : £500–£600)
(Won in competition with contestants from the whole country. Owing to the high standard required, this was the only scholarship awarded by the school in two years.)

★ Cheltenham College
★ St. Swithun's
★ Talbot Heath, Bournemouth
★ Queenswood
★ Embley Park
★ Stamford High School
★ Kenderick School, Reading
★ St. Margaret's
★ Chichester High School
★ Royal School, Bath

Holiday Coaching
1 Common Entrance to King's School, Canterbury

RESULTS SPEAK FOR THEMSELVES

Teachers include Oxford and Cambridge Graduates

BROOMBANK SCHOOL
MANOR ROAD, SELSEY
SELSEY : 2774

The oldest established Preparatory School in Selsey

A Boarding and Day School for Boys and Girls (aged 4–14) with a Coaching Class for older children preparing for Cambridge University and the General Certificate of Education.

The School is situated in spacious and most beautiful surroundings.

PRINCIPALS :
W. P. HIGGS, M.A., Mus.B.(Cantab), F.R.C.O., Lafontaine Prize.
Mrs. W. P. HIGGS, M.S.I.A.

UNDER DISTINGUISHED PATRONAGE

51. Advertisement for Broombank School, *c.*1954.

Chapter Ten

Transport through the Ages

Any elderly Selsey resident asked to reminisce on this subject would almost certainly begin with the Selsey tramway, known as the 'Bumpity Bump' and surely one of the oddest railways ever to have existed. This Heath Robinson affair was later to be the subject of many comic postcards. The first railway reached Chichester from Brighton in 1846 and was soon extended to Portsmouth. In 1896 the Light Railways Act was passed, enabling local lines to be constructed cheaply by condoning lower safety standards, though this was compensated for by severe speed restrictions. At about the same time a group of influential local people met to consider the construction of a railway from Chichester to Selsey. Landowners were willing to sell land, especially if they were promised a railway siding close to their farm, because the coming of rail transport increased land values. However, the tramway was soon nicknamed 'the Hedgerow Railway' because the line hugged the hedges so that the minimum possible land would need to be bought! A tramway company – the Hundred of Manhood and Selsey Tramway Company – was formed in Selsey instead of a railway company, partly because railway companies were subject to more restrictive legislation and partly because tramways could operate across public highways without special safety precautions being taken at level crossings. The guard or fireman would just stand in the middle of the road to stop all motor traffic!

The gauge was to be the same as the L.B. & S.C.R., 4 ft. 8½ in., and the originators of the project stated that 'it was not intended or desired to run trains at express speeds' – they certainly spoke the truth in that instance! An estimated £12,000 capital was needed and it was hoped that a large part would be supplied by Chichester residents. No government aid was sought, and no parliamentary sanction was given for the building of this tramway. Mr. H. F. Stephens (later Lieutenant-Colonel), of Tonbridge and London, who had already carried out similar work elsewhere, was appointed Engineer. The route was practically level throughout, so no great engineering works were necessary, except at the canal bridge at Hunston where water had to be pumped out so that the concrete foundations for the track could be laid.

One hundred men were employed to lay the line, working from both the Chichester and Selsey ends. It was completed within four months, in spite of a short strike – on 2 September 1897 *The West Sussex Gazette* reported, 'The whole of the workmen employed on the Selsey railway left their work on Tuesday in consequence of the contractor lowering their wages a halfpenny an hour'. Industrial action is by no means a new phenomenon! A district which had previously had to rely on horse-drawn transport was now able to enjoy the benefits of steam-powered locomotion. This had long been needed, both for the transportation of agricultural products from the Sidlesham area and fish from Selsey and also to bring the increasing number of summer visitors into Selsey, already developing as a seaside resort. Prior to this time anyone wishing to travel from Selsey to Chichester had three choices: a leisurely walk, a ride on a privately-owned horse or pony and trap, or a ride in one of the carriers' vans. The journey was by no means fast, as the carrier would call at wayside farm cottages to pick up orders for provisions, and the return trip usually included stops at the hostelries along the way! James Pett was listed as a carrier as early as the 1841 census and by 1886 William Fidler, John James, James Pett and John Pink were all listed in *Pike's Directory* as carriers.

52. A donkey-drawn carriage in Selsey in the 1890s.

53. Fidler's horse-drawn carrier's waggon outside the *New Inn* (now the *Neptune*), *c.*1912. Note all the holidaymakers' luggage on the back of the waggon. William Michael Fidler is sitting in the trap, Charles Fidler is standing by the waggon and Jack Norris, a delivery boy, is standing by the horse's head.

Fidler's carrier service had been founded by Michael Fidler (1823-82), a Master Mariner who had spent many years at sea in the merchant navy. At the time of the 1871 census Michael, his wife Jane and their four children, including William Michael, aged nine and classifed as a carrier's boy, were living at 'Arnell's House' in Selsey. The carrier's business flourished and by the time William Michael was 16, he had joined his father as a junior partner. The company had about fifteen horses which pulled the large carrier's vans. William Fidler took over a well-established business on his father's death and soon purchased premises in Grafton Road. At the end of the First World War he bought a motor lorry in an effort to cope with the growing number of holiday-makers who visited the village during the summer months.

The first traffic used the 7½ miles of tramway on 27 August 1897, but stopped 200 yards short of Selsey Town Station (at Manor Farm), the building of which was not finished in time for the opening. Selsey was en fête for the occasion and a special lunch was served at Beacon House. The train arrived very late from Chichester and unpunctuality was the tramway's keynote for the next 35 years. In 1898 the line was extended another half mile to the beach. Severe coastal erosion brought the beach closer to the station each year and fishermen were able to despatch their crabs and lobsters very conveniently when the trains came as far as the beach during the summer months. During the First World War this part was closed, the track removed and never restored. The total cost of constructing the line, including land purchase, amounted to £21,570 and £3,268 was spent in the first instance on rolling stock. But profits were soon being made and the tramway showed every sign of being a prosperous enterprise.

54. The *Sidlesham* in action, *c.*1908.

55. 'The new Selsey tram', brought into operation after the flooding of 1910. The coach is standing at the junction of Chichester Road and Rookery Lane at Sidlesham. The driver is Harry Prior and the passengers sat on top of the coach to avoid getting wet when the horses pulled it through the floods and water covered the floor of the coach.

The route taken by the tram was Chichester, Hunston, Hoe Farm (a private station), Chalder Farm, Mill Pond Halt, Sidlesham, Ferry, the Golf Club Halt (also private), Selsey Bridge, Selsey Town and Selsey Beach. Eleven stations or halts on a line only eight miles long must constitute some sort of record. Simple timber and corrugated iron buildings were erected at all stations except Hoe Farm and Golf Club Halts, though Selsey Town Station was more elaborate, with a waiting room, booking office and superintendent's office. Only the stations at Chichester, Hunston and Selsey were staffed. The wooden locomotive shed, capable of housing six locomotives, was situated at the east end of Selsey Station and was used for repairing rolling stock. In the early years of this century the *Crown Inn* had livery stables and coachmen used to ride to meet the tram to collect passengers and provisions for the shops. The Crown Riding Stables were listed in *Kelly's Directory* for 1930, with Cripps Bros. as proprietors.

Disaster struck on the night of 10 December 1910 when the sea broke through its bank on the eastern side of the peninsula, covering two miles of track between Chalder and Ferry with water 12 ft. deep in places. Sidlesham station itself was flooded at high tide, the water being above the platform. Fortunately the company was in a sufficiently sound financial position to be able to pay the estimated £2,500 for the construction of a mile-long embankment up to 15 ft. high to carry the line across the flooded Pagham Harbour. While the work was in progress, a horse-drawn bus was used to convey passengers from Ferry to Mill Pond Halt.

The period up to the First World War was the hey-day of the little railway. Soon afterwards there was a decline in passenger traffic using the tramway because of the increase

56. Maidment's cycle shop in the High Street in the 1920s. Lewis Maidment (known as Gus) is standing in front of the shop behind the motorcycles. He advertised himself as a saddler and harness maker, too.

57a. Maidment's garage in the High Street, *c.*1950. The pumps on the pavement were installed in 1924. The road looks strangely deserted by comparison with the 1980s.

in the number of private motor cars. By the 1920s H. J. Blake was advertising his taxi service in Manor Road, and William Fidler's carrier's service was now motorised. His first petrol-driven lorry was an ex-U.S. Army five-ton 'Selden' with solid tyres. This was soon joined by a Model 'T' Ford and later by two Morris Commercial five-ton lorries. William Fidler died in 1933 at the age of 71. William's son Charles Fidler took over the business. In 1965 he recalled for a newspaper interview, 'We used to pick up passengers and goods at the Neptune, Selsey, leaving there at 9 in the morning and taking 2 hours over the journey into Chichester, returning at 4 in the afternoon'. W. Fidler & Son's carrier trade finally ceased in 1938 when Charles suffered a heart attack, brought about to a large extent by the Road Traffic Act of 1930 which caused problems for carriers throughout Britain by introducing a system of licensing for any public vehicle plying for trade and regulating the construction and weight of such vehicles.

The appearance of three garages in Selsey bears witness to the increase in the number of motor vehicles in the village. These were Central Garage, with Mr. H. T. Chambers as proprietor, the Selsey Motor and Engineering Company, and Maidment's Garage, all in the High Street. Lewis Maidment (1873-1946) had begun his career in about 1909 as a cycle agent in East Street but moved with the times and by 1927 was advertising himself as an automobile engineer. By the 1930s he could claim to be the official motor car and motor cycle repairer to the R.A.C. and had accommodation for 60 cars in his spacious garage. Unlike the tramway, Maidment's and Chambers' Garages were still operating in the 1950s.

Another blow to the tramway (and of course the carriers) was the commencement of a rival bus service, more convenient than the tram as it ran into the centre of Chichester and throughout the sprawling village of Selsey. The Southdown Company[27] started regular bus services in July 1920 with five return journeys a day, and by 1924 there were 12 journeys each way on weekdays and nine on Sundays. The bus left from Chichester station and, once it reached Selsey, stopped at Station Road, Manor Road, East Street, High Street and Hillfield Road (the *Marine Hotel*). The journey took about 45 minutes. In the 1920s the vehicles were very rudimentary, petrol-electric buses with solid tyres and the driver in his unscreened seat would have had to contend with wind and rain, and at night the darkness would have been pierced only by feebly wavering oil-burning lamps. There had in fact been an earlier Chichester and Selsey Motor Omnibus Company but this survived for only three years, operating from 1906 to 1909. Early in the 1920s two Selsey men, Col. W. G. Moore and Capt. Fuller, began a private bus service for the village, running two red buses from Col. Moore's garage situated where Jackson's Garage is today. This was quickly taken over by the Southdown Company. In 1946 a second service was introduced, starting from West Street in Chichester, and travelling via Donnington rather than Hunston, arriving in Seal Road, Selsey, 35 minutes later. This service ran hourly seven days a week at the outset, but the Sunday morning services were curtailed later. By the 1950s there was a half-hourly bus link with Chichester on weekdays and an hourly service on Sundays; this continued right up to the 1970s. The two services, originally 52 and 52A, have since been renumbered 250 and 251 respectively.

A census of traffic was taken over a period of seven days in August 1923. The number of vehicles travelling in and out of Selsey totalled 3,840 motors of various sorts, 365 horse-drawn vehicles, 2,337 bicycles and 20 buses each day.

The tramway began to be ridiculed in the 1920s as engines refused to start in the mornings and were late reaching their destination more often than not. Trains were late for a variety of reasons ranging from the guard oversleeping to cows wandering along the line or the loss of steam at crucial points. Whenever it was wet, the steam train had great difficulty in climbing the slope up to Kipson Bank at Hunston because of the slippery rails, and then passengers had to get out and walk up the track to the top. The comic postcards were not

MAIDMENT'S
GARAGE (Next to Post Office)

Accommodation for 60 Cars
Repairs of every discription
: All Accessories in Stock :
: : Cars for Hire : :
Motor and Cycle Agents
All leading makes supplied

High St. & Lewes Rd.,
SELSEY

Telegrams: Maidment, Selsey.
Telephone: Selsey 33

57b. Maidment's advertisement, *c.*1930.

58. A Southdown bus venturing through floodwater at Ferry, November 1931. This was a common sight until the concrete road was built.

far removed from the reality! All too frequently, long-suffering teachers in Chichester had to accept with a smile the all-too-familiar excuse from Selsey children, 'The train was late, Miss'. At best, because of all the stops at level crossings, the train took 39 minutes to do the eight miles in 1924.

Cheap summer excursions were run from Selsey to other south coast resorts such as Brighton, Worthing, Littlehampton, Bognor, Hayling Island and Portsmouth. The return fare to Brighton was 5s. 6d. first class, and 4s. 0d. second class, in 1912. There were no different class rides on the normal Selsey to Chichester route (7½d. single, 1s. 3d. return, children under 12 half price and children under three free of charge in 1913), but for an extra 3d. for the single journey, a passenger could travel in a saloon.

Many locomotives ran on the line over the years. The *Selsey*, a 2-4-2 side tank, was the only one to be specially built for the line, being acquired in 1897 and withdrawn with badly leaking boiler tubes only six months before the tramway ceased to operate. The other locomotives had been in use on other lines before arriving in Selsey – *Chichester I* (built in 1847 and therefore an old lady before she began work on the tramway), *Sidlesham*, *Hesperus*, *Chichester II*, *Ringing Rock* and *Morous*. In February 1928 an alternative method of locomotion was tried in the form of two Shefflex rail cars joined together back to back, each seating 23 passengers. These were powered by four-cylinder petrol engines and luggage could be carried on the top of the cars. They proved very economical to run so two Ford cars were later bought, but those travelling inside suffered from exhaust fumes and had a very bumpy ride.

The only fatal accident on the tramway occurred in September 1923 when the 8.15 a.m. train from Selsey jumped the rails near Golf Club Halt, plunged down a bank and all three coaches were derailed. The fireman, H. Barnes, was killed instantly and the driver sustained serious scalds. All traffic on the line had to be suspended for two days. At the time of the derailment the train had been travelling at its usual speed of about 16 m.p.h. A verdict of accidental death was given at the inquest on the fireman, but the jury expressed the opinion that the Chief Engineer and the Company were indirectly to blame as there was evidence of neglect in the upkeep of the track – many people believed that the rails had spread and the engine dropped between them. A police constable giving evidence said that he had been unable to find even one completely sound sleeper at the scene of the mishap. Accidents frequently occurred at level crossings. In 1932 a Minister of Transport Inspector enquired into a collision at Stockbridge Road and asked why the crossing had never been inspected. He was apparently satisfied with the explanation that the line was a tramway and not a railway.

This was not strictly true by 1932 since in 1924 the directors of the tramway, anxious about its declining fortunes, decided that they should form themselves into a railway company, perhaps to encourage the newly-created Southern Railway to take over the line. This did not happen, however, and the conversion of the tramway to a railway (the West Sussex Light Railway) by the stroke of a pen did nothing to halt the steady decline in passenger figures. In 1919 there had been 102,292 passengers, bringing in receipts of £3,912 13s. 0d.; by 1924 there were only 31,352 passengers; and by 1930 a mere 15,904, receipts having slumped to the alarmingly low level of £354 4s. 11d. In 1933 the single fare between Selsey and Chichester was only 8d. but this failed to attract passengers who preferred to pay 11d. to the Southdown Motor Company for greater comfort and reliability of service. The tram fare was impossibly low – the Southern Railway would have charged 11½d. for a journey of the same length. In the summer of 1913 there had been 11 trains a day each way, by 1917 there were only six, with four on Sundays. By 1934 the Sunday service had been suspended altogether.

59. The *Sidlesham* at Selsey station, before 1926. In the early days the station had a domed roof but by 1926 this had been replaced by a pitched one (*see* no. 63).

60. A Shefflex railway car on the tramline, photographed at Ferry.

61. Derailment of the locomotive *Wembley*, later renamed *Chichester*, near Selsey Golf Links, 3 September 1923.

62. The *Morous* crossing the road at Ferry in the 1920s. Many accidents and 'near misses' occurred on this part of the line as there were no signals or crossing gates. The sign on the left merely requests 'All Trains Stop Here'.

63. Selsey station photographed in April 1926.

Fortunately, freight traffic remained steady, yielding an income of around £2,000 during the years after the First World War. In 1933 this included almost £720 for unspecified goods (including milk, bricks, stone, chalk, cement, lime, corn, manure and timber), £167 for minerals, almost £700 for coal and coke, £260 for parcels, £15 for livestock and £41 for mail and parcel post (charged according to weight). Parcels were carried to Selsey for the G.P.O. by tram well into the 1930s.

Selsey had never had a mail coach service. In November 1825 James N. Palmer, then Rector of Selsey, wrote to enquire about the possibility of establishing a daily postal service between Chichester and Selsey

> upon payment of a subscription of two Guineas per ann. and an additional charge of one penny upon all letters brought in and carried out . . . To such an arrangement my Parishioners would be very willing to agree for we suffer greatly here both from uncertainty and infrequency in the delivery of letters – Chichester our Post Town being eight miles off we depend almost entirely upon the Carriers, who during the winter half of the year go there but twice a week and who are not always careful to deliver them as soon as they get them into their possession – and indeed in the ordinary course of things we *never* receive a letter until Twenty four hours after its arrival at the Chichester Office – and in no case can we answer by return of post.

An investigation was made by the Post Office into the feasibility of a daily postal service. It was reported in May 1826 that there was such a small volume of correspondence and newspapers sent to 'Donnington, Siddlesham and Selsea' each week that the expenditure involved in establishing a daily mail coach service could not be justified, 'either by a Messenger from Chichester, or by an extension of the present Post from Bognor to Aldwick'.

The operations of the tramway must have been a great boon to those people in Selsey who wrote letters frequently.

Returning to the 1930s, tramway expenditure on wages was not great: for example, 13s. per week for a lad porter, £1 for a guard-conductor, £3 3s. 0d. for a fitter driver, £2 for a fireman labourer and £2 12s. 1d. for a rail-car driver. These wages were paid for a nominal 54-hour week, which included working until 9 p.m. on Saturdays and 11 p.m. on Wednesdays! Even so, by 1933 there was a massive debt of £5,274 in debenture interest and £7,467 owing to the executors of Colonel Stephens, always referred to on the line as 'the Colonel'. It was probably these debts which prevented the Southern Railway from showing an interest in the line. Stephens had become a director and eventually the major shareholder of the Selsey tramway company. His great skill as an engineer made him much sought after by directors of other minor railways and he eventually controlled a dozen or more lines. He died in 1931 before his empire began to crumble.

Services on the Selsey line finally ceased on 19 January 1935 – there had only been one train a day during the previous eight weeks. Unfortunately, the Selsey locomotives had become notorious for unpunctuality in their later years. As well as halting at level crossings, the train would be stopped for the guard to deal with animals which frequently strayed on to the line, or to walk to farms along the line to enquire if the farmer wanted the train to pick up any produce the following day. Songs were even written ridiculing the service:

> If you live at Sidlesham and do not keep a car,
> And you want to go to Chichester the journey isn't far
> The journey is quite simple, the miles they are but few,
> If you leave at ten o'clock, you may get there by two.
>
> *Chorus*
> The Sidlesham Snail, the Sidlesham Snail,
> The boiler's burst, she's off the rail.

64. Postcard issued by the Cynicus Publishing Co. Ltd. – a comment on the speed at which the Selsey tram travelled. Although the men and women helping to push are true to life, there were never signals or a signal box on the line.

It is sad, however, to think of a line closing after 38 hectic years of serving the people of Selsey, and of the 12 employees who received their final wage packets in January 1935. The line and the rolling stock were put up for sale by tender. Everything was purchased for £3,610, insufficient to pay off the mortgage and debenture holders, who received only a small percentage of their holdings. Little evidence of the tramway remains today, only fragments of the platform edge at Hunston and Chalder, a chalk embankment in Pagham Harbour and a hummock just north of the Fishermen's Beach huts where as late as 1958 the steps and platform of the Selsey Beach station could be seen. The station building at Selsey Town was dismantled by German prisoners of war in December 1946. However, a permanent reminder is the public house, the *Selsey Tram*, just south of Chichester at Donnington and not far from the old route.

Chapter Eleven

Selsey in War and Peace

Selsey, like towns up and down the country, began making preparations for war and for defence before hostilities broke out in August 1914. In December 1913 'G' Company (Chichester) of the Territorials of the Royal Sussex Regiment visited Selsey and paraded through the village with a view to recruiting. Afterwards 15 Selseyites did indeed offer themselves for service to king and country and joined the Territorials. By July 1914 there were rumours that Selsey was to be chosen as one of the stations for the government to base an aeroplane for use by the coastguard service in conjunction with the Royal Flying Corps. During the same month the King inspected destroyer patrol flotillas anchored between Selsey and Littlehampton, on their way to the Solent for review.

In September 1914 *The Chichester Observer* published the names of local men on active service. Under Selsey, 52 names were given for naval service, 35 for military service and 11 for the Territorials. It was stressed that this list was not comprehensive and it was updated in later editions of the newspaper. In October 1914 an evening of variety entertainment to promote recruiting was held in the cinema hall – a programme of war films and patriotic songs, organised by Archibald Hamilton, the Recruiting Officer for Selsey and district. A similar programme of entertainments had been put on by the Manhood Minstrels in the public hall (*see* page 135) many years before, in February 1900, in aid of a relief fund for the widows and children of soldiers killed in the Boer War. In December 1914 the women of the village met together to advance the work of the Ladies' Linen League for the Royal West Sussex Hospital and at Christmas the soldiers and coastguards stationed in Selsey were given dinner by the villagers in the cinema hall, and were then entertained with a programme of music. By Christmas 1914 Archibald Hamilton was able to report with pride that there were only 25 able-bodied young men in the village who had not joined the colours and, of these, 10 were in the National Reserve.

Sir Archibald Hamilton, born in 1876, was the eldest son of Sir Edward Hamilton, Bart., of Iping House, Midhurst, and a direct descendant of Lord Nelson's Lady Hamilton. He succeeded to the family baronetcy on his father's death in 1915. He was a great local character and in the years after the war often paraded through the village, dressed in his kilt, preceded by a piper, and heralded by strong fumes of eucalyptus, his private health cure. In 1924 this colourful character, earlier President of the Selsey branch of the Conservative Association, claimed to have become a Mohammedan and announced his intention of making a pilgrimage to Mecca one day. He lived at Paisley Cottage in Seal Square. The elaborately decorated black and white house, formerly known as The Gables, is still standing today, behind its barricade of black, gold and blue painted iron gates.

In March 1915 the first death in action of a Selsey parishioner was reported – William Henry Woolven, who had lived in Upper Norton, was among the casualties of the Dardanelles operation. He and Cecil John Colton of the 2nd Battalion Royal Sussex Regiment, killed near La Bassée, were remembered in a special memorial service at the conclusion of evensong at Selsey parish church in May 1915. Such services were repeated with sad regularity throughout the war. Norton churchyard now has memorials to several local men killed in this war, including brothers Dudley and Edward Jewell, and P. E. Soloman who was killed in October 1915 at the tragically young age of 20 on H.M. Drifter *Star of Buchan*.

The war affected everyone, civilians as well as those serving in the armed forces, and children as well as adults. Red Cross and Stretcher Bearer classes were organised in the village and in June 1915 the United Methodist church held its Sunday School anniversary, with a flower service, sports, games and tea in a field near the mill. The traditional outing to Goodwood was foregone by the children and the money saved was sent to the Belgian Relief Fund. The annual meeting of the Manhood Red Cross Aid Society held in October 1915 reported that there were by then 400 members and that since the society had been formed over 1,950 garments had been made or given by members, as well as 26 bags of swabs and 20 sandbags. These were all distributed among the British Red Cross in London, Belgian refugees in England, Chichester Base Hospital Stores, the local coastguards and local men on the front. In June 1917 a Food Economy Campaign meeting was held at the cinema hall, a speaker from London impressing on her Selsey audience the necessity for economy in wheat flour and cereals in particular.

In September 1916 *The Chichester Observer* reported a more 'local' Zeppelin raid than any previous attack, though the newspaper was not permitted to print full details. Several hostile airships had visited the southern counties during the night and people had been

65. Each Christmas during the First World War, soldiers and coastguards stationed in Selsey were given a celebration dinner by the residents of the village. It was held in the cinema hall, suitably decorated with flags, and the troops were entertained by a programme of vocal and instrumental music. A music stand can be seen in the background of this photograph, taken at Christmas 1916. Many of the men on that occasion were members of the 9th Hampshire Cycle Regiment, employed on coastal defence.

awakened by the firing of guns. The fire brigade and special constables turned out in case of emergency, but their services were not required as there were no casualties or damage to property in the area. In May 1917 restrictions were introduced for fishing boats and pleasure cruisers – at Selsey pleasure craft were forbidden to go outside a one-mile radius from the coastguard station.

Many Selsey men were killed during the First World War, so it is no wonder that the peace celebration in July 1919 was such a noisy and welcome event. All the houses in the village were decorated with flags, brightly-coloured paper, material and even handkerchiefs. Some local children turned up dressed entirely in flags. There was a short thanksgiving service in St Peter's church, followed by sports held in the meadow, tea in a barn and then an evening concert in the cinema hall. People walked the streets, letting off fireworks, singing, shouting and thoroughly enjoying themselves in spite of the heavy rain. The evening concluded with a bonfire on the beach. A Peace Dinner was given at the cinema hall in September 1919, the menu cards bearing the following words: 'The inhabitants of Selsey offer you a hearty welcome home and thank you for having done your share towards obtaining the Great Victory'. It was reported that 300 Selsey men had gone out on active service and that over 50 had been killed.

66. The war memorial erected in St Peter's churchyard in 1920.

They were not to be forgotten, however. In January 1920 a public meeting was held to discuss a memorial cross to be erected in the churchyard. It was agreed that the design should be similar to the Saxon crosses erected by St Wilfrid. The four ancient carved stones, believed to have formed part of the original Selsey cross in the seventh century, were to be incorporated into the new cross. The £500 needed for the memorial was raised by voluntary contributions. The cross, made of Portland stone, was built at the edge of the churchyard facing the High Street. It was 18 ft. high and the names of the 55 fallen were inscribed on panels at the base. The unveiling and dedication ceremony took place in May 1921, on Whit Sunday. Rev. K. H. MacDermott (who had himself served as army chaplain in the Balkans during the war) and Rev. Frank Dennis (minister of the United Methodist church) officiated, and His Grace the Duke of Richmond and Gordon unveiled the cross.

Selsey quickly resumed its normal peacetime activities once the war was over. To some it may have seemed something of a backwater, cut off from the rest of the country by its geographical location at the tip of a peninsula and with only one road from Chichester leading in and out of the village. Selsey has never been on a through-route to any other place and has therefore maintained something of its earlier insularity. It was precisely this insularity which attracted many famous people to Selsey in the years between the war. Actors and singers found in Selsey the peace and relative anonymity they longed for as a respite from the pressures of their lives in the public eye in London and other great cities. Some made Selsey their permanent home and others spent long summer holidays in the village each year with their families, enjoying the sun, the sea and the golden sands.

67. Children enjoying themselves on the sands, *c.*1930. This photograph was taken on Marine Beach (the *Marine Hotel* would be just to the right of the picture), an area of golden sands until the groynes were built and shingle began to collect. In the background on the right are beach huts, a few of the 40 or so owned by Don Hunnisett and hired out for changing. The boat on the beach would probably have been one of his also.

Eric Coates (1886-1957) was one of those who chose to make Selsey his home in his later years. He was a great composer, starting his career as leading violinist in the Queen's Hall Orchestra under Sir Henry Wood, who produced several of his early compositions at Promenade concerts. After 1918 Coates devoted himself entirely to composing light music, including 'The Three Bears' (1926), 'The London Suite' (1933), the suites 'Four Centuries' (1941) and 'The Three Elizabeths' (1944), and a number of popular waltzes and marches. He conducted his own works in many countries. In the early 1930s he bought a house (named as 'Summer Days' in *Kelly's Directory* for 1934) on the corner of Hillfield Road and

Latham Road, where he lived with his wife Phyllis and son Austin, though they had earlier taken a bungalow in The Crescent, East Beach. Their last home on the peninsula was at Sidlesham, and Coates died in Chichester in 1957.

Another equally famous Selsey resident between the wars was Tom Walls (1883-1949), the actor, director and theatre manager. He is perhaps best known for the long succession of 'Aldwych Farces' which he directed and in which he also acted. He always played the role of the flashy opportunist, teamed with Ralph Lynn's 'silly ass' and Robertson Hare's bewildered 'little man'. Tom Walls lived in a house off Danefield Road, named in *Kelly's Directory* for 1938 as 'Sandcott'. This house has survived into the 1980s. Both Hare and Lynn were frequent visitors to Selsey while Walls lived here. The Aldwych Farces included one called 'Rookery Nook', actually written in Selsey where there was a house called 'The Rookery' in Beach Road. Tom Walls owned a horse called 'April the Fifth', a brown colt which won the Derby in 1932. His owner collected £9,730 in prize money and many locals backed the horse. *The Daily Mail* ran a story on 'April the Fifth' in August 1932 – the horse had been favourite for the St Leger race until it was announced at Goodwood that he had leg trouble and was taking a course of sea baths at Selsey! 'April' trained on Selsey sands and was stabled in a barn in the village, near to where Chambers Garage used to be. Tom Walls is well remembered by elderly Selsey residents for his Rolls Royce as well as his famous horse.

R. C. Sherriff (1896-1975) wrote the famous and moving play, *Journey's End*, in the house of that name still in Manor Road, opposite the *Selsey Hotel*, in 1928. The play dealt with the reactions of a small group of men in a dug-out just before an attack during the First World War. *Journey's End* was subsequently translated and played all over the world, being first seen in New York in 1929. Sherriff had the house built for his mother but spent a lot of time there himself, especially during the summer months. At the back of the house was a wide balcony with views of the sea – surely an inspiration for Sherriff when writing his many scripts for theatre plays. Another author, Jerome K. Jerome, lived in 'Klapka' at 27 James Street for some years. Jerome's own middle name was Klapka. Born in 1858, he is best remembered for his great work, *Three Men in a Boat*, which was written in 1889 and conveys the ecstasy of summer holidays. Perhaps it is a record of summers spent by Jerome and two friends in Selsey. Harold Williams, born in Sydney in 1893, also lived in Selsey in the inter-war years. He was an operatic and concert baritone who toured Australia and New Zealand and was one of the first opera singers to broadcast on British radio. He lived in a house in Hillfield Road, appropriately named 'Boomerang'.

Many other stars of the stage were regular summer visitors to Selsey. These included Bud Flanagan (1896-1968) and Chesney Allen (1894-1982), the popular singing and comedy double act team which was part of the Crazy Gang. They appeared together frequently at the London Palladium in the 1930s and at the Victoria Palace up until 1960. Flanagan and Allen visited Selsey for several summers, bringing their children who rode at Miss Scrimgeour's stables in West Street. Sophie Tucker (1884-1966) was another singer who made frequent visits to the village. She was an American vaudeville artiste, well known on the British music hall stage as 'the last of the Red Hot Mommas'. She appeared frequently at the London Palladium and at London Variety performances both before and after the Second World War, and became famous for her tear-jerker, 'My Yiddisher Momma'. During her annual visits to Selsey she often put on shows in the Pavilion (cinema hall). Bransby Williams (1870-1961), another star of the British music hall, stayed in Selsey during long summer holidays. He had a large repertory of comic characters from Dickens's novels and also specialised in dramatic monologues with a musical accompaniment, of which the best known was 'The Green Eye of the Little Yellow God'. In 1904 he had been commanded to

Sandringham to play before Edward VII, and he made many successful appearances in America.

The Crossley family of vehicle manufacturers also lived in Selsey at this time (*see* page 35), as did more local celebrities, still remembered with affection today. These included 'Charlie' Morgan, 'Granny' Willis and Pat Wills-Rust. 'Charlie' Morgan died in May 1928 and was sadly missed by Selsey folk. For many years he had lived in a caravan near Medmerry Mill with horses and dogs as his sole companions. In his younger days he had lost both his legs in an accident, but made light of his handicap, hobbling about on his remaining stumps. He earned his living by doing odd jobs and dealing in horses. He was invariably cheerful and is remembered for the wonderful way he had with animals. Mrs. Ann Willis, affectionately known as 'Granny' Willis, celebrated her 100th birthday in January 1932, receiving the customary telegram from the king. She had lived in the Selsey district all her life, having been born in Sidlesham. A birthday party was held for her in the church hall and she walked there from her home and returned on foot afterwards. She finally died in January 1934, just three days before her 102nd birthday. She had been the oldest resident in a district renowned for the longevity of its inhabitants, and attributed her long life to 'hard work and no worry'. Pat Wills-Rust (1906-75) was a naval man, remembered for his tattoos and the huge rings he wore. His mother, Miss Wills, was a member of the famous tobacco family which made Selsey their home for some years.

All too soon, however, the peace and tranquility which had attracted so many well-known people to Selsey was violently shattered and it became clear that the 1914-18 conflict had not been 'the war to end wars'. Older residents of the village remember Oswald Mosley, who founded the British Union of Fascists in 1932, parading with his Blackshirts on West Beach on Sundays. Mosley certainly lived locally, in Honer, just south of Mundham, and the Blackshirts held summer camps at Honer Farm. They also camped at Wakely's Mill in Medmerry and drove into Selsey in their armoured cars, fully uniformed and in their jackboots. Mosley made impassioned speeches from a box outside Large Acres (near Wiseman's today). A few Selsey men were themselves Blackshirts and disappeared from the village when war was declared. In July 1934 a crowd gathered at the Pavilion (cinema hall) as the policy of the B.U.F. was explained to Selsey residents, invited to the meeting there by Sir Archibald Hamilton who arrived escorted as usual by the Rob Roy Pipers.[28] During the summer of 1938 all the villagers were issued with gas masks and as soon as war was declared in September 1939 holidaymakers packed their bags and left Selsey in droves. Activity on the sea increased and troopships, supplyships and warships could be seen daily, sailing to or from Portsmouth around the Nab Head.

Soon there were more and more indications that the war was no 'phoney war'. On 31 July 1939 *The Evening News* reported on an R.A.F. training camp to be held at Church Norton during that week. Over the weekend about 250 boys from 35 of the biggest public schools had arrived for a week under canvas, trained by some of their masters who held commissions in the Auxiliary Air Force. Officers of the regular R.A.F. were also present to give expert tuition. The camp was held in the flying field of Norton Priory, by permission of its owner, Major Norman Holden, and close to Pagham Harbour where bathing parties were held. The cadets visited Tangmere for a demonstration of low-level attacks and dive bombing by a squadron of battle aircraft. Before long a searchlight battery was stationed near Bill House as well as an anti-aircraft battery on the farmland to the west of the Mill. These were soon followed by a detachment of mechanised troops with their Bren-carriers. One of the earliest local casualties in the war was 19-year-old Alan Abery, killed in action on H.M.S. *Cossack* which was landing troops at Narvik when she came under fire from shore-based German guns and Stuka dive-bombers.

68. Concrete defence blocks at Medmerry: these were erected during the Second World War.

69. The burnt-out remains of a Heinkel III which crashed in Selsey on 11 July 1940.

In July 1940 a German reconnaissance plane, a Heinkel III, made a forced landing at the north end of Park Copse, her engines having been disabled by a Spitfire's guns. The Heinkel had been taking part in a raid on Portsmouth and Solent shipping and its flight had been monitored by the new Radio-Location unit in the field near Broadreeds holiday camp. One German crewman was dead, another called Willi Muller died on the beach and is buried in Tangmere, while the pilot and a fourth man were taken prisoner. The local constable was later left to guard the plane but after a few days villagers congregated and helped themselves to useful items from the wreckage – the tail wheel was taken for use on a wheelbarrow and the perspex disappeared from the cabins and soon re-appeared in the form of jewellery in the windows of enterprising shopkeepers!

Children from up and down the country were evacuated to the holiday camp in Selsey for safety and were visited in the village by the Queen Mother. The evacuees were later moved on when Selsey itself was bombed.

Selsey, like other towns on the south coast, was particularly vulnerable when the Germans gained control of the French coast in June 1940 and there were constant enemy air raids preparatory to the launching of an invasion by sea. In fact Selsey suffered more air raids than any other place in Sussex. Up until 3 September 1942, Selsey heard 939 air raid sirens warning of enemy aircraft overhead. After that date the A.R.P. ceased to keep a record of every 'red warning'. The German 9th Army planned to send troops from the Le Havre area and land them in the vicinity of Brighton. They would then spread out towards Selsey Bill in the west and Bexhill in the east. At that time the flat south coast was virtually undefended, with no anti-tank traps, barbed wire, mined beaches or other obstacles against enemy landing craft and troops. As a first priority the War Office decided to establish emergency defence batteries along the coast. In West Sussex these were sited about seven miles apart. Such a battery was established at Aldwick. An anti-tank barrier was built along the coastline at Selsey – huge concrete blocks, each six feet high, were cast *in situ* and the grass in front was wired and mined. The beaches were fenced off and closed to the public and East Beach was eventually occupied entirely by troops, with a sentry on duty at the top of Park Lane. The beaches, scene of so much innocent joy in more peaceful times, were riddled with barbed wire, tank traps and mines.

Selsey's fishermen were almost all away in the Navy, as were the coastguards, but the village was full of assorted British and allied troops, armoured cars, gun carriers and tanks, and most civilians were involved in war work of some kind – with the Women's Voluntary Service, the Red Cross (stationed in the Rectory for most of the war), the fire brigade, or as Air Raid Wardens. Mrs. Vera Buxton Knight of Vincent Road, Selsey's A.R.P. during the war, was also Transport Officer for the Red Cross and St John Ambulance Brigade. These organisations helped save the lives of eight airmen, some British and some German, shot down off the coast, then rescued by the Selsey lifeboat and given first aid treatment before being taken to hospital in Chichester. This civilian work could be very dangerous. On one occasion Mrs. Buxton Knight led a stretcher party through a minefield on the West Beach to try to rescue some British soldiers who had wandered across it by mistake and detonated one of the mines; unfortunately they were all killed. The village itself was a closed area, many houses having been requisitioned for troops from other parts of Britain, America or Canada. American servicemen, for example, took over the *Marine Hotel* for the duration of the war and members of the Canadian Air Force were billeted at the Manor House.

In August 1940 the Selsey Spitfire Fund was launched. It was hoped to raise £5,000 for a spitfire to be named 'The Selsey Bill'. The fund was organised by Mrs. Buxton Knight. Many local shops sold 'Spitfire buttons' at a minimum price of sixpence, residents gave generous donations and many enterprising fund-raising activities were held including auctions, boxing tournaments, dances and an exhibition of locally-collected German relics.

70. The first house in Selsey to be hit by a bomb during the Second World War, the Homer's house in Hillfield Road.

71. Aerial view of the crater, 64 ft. x 64 ft. x 16 ft. deep, on the golf course, made by a parachute mine on 26 June 1941.

In 1940 the Selsey Local Defence Volunteers (later called the Home Guard) were organised by a retired army colonel named Egerton. Thirty men and boys, too young to enlist in the regular army, were issued with hoes, rakes and pitchforks, and were taught rudimentary drill and to make petrol bombs. A rota was organised so that men could keep guard on key points in the village – the gasworks, water tower, telephone exchange and the beach. They were supplied with battle dress and tin hats. After a month or so, because Selsey was considered particularly vulnerable, the men were issued with real firearms, Lee Enfield rifles, two officers' pistols and a Browning machine gun. A field near Broad Rife was used for target practice and the men dug gun emplacements at strategic points along the coast from Church Norton to Bracklesham.

During the Battle of Britain the L.D.V.s rushed to their appointed places, day or night. On several occasions German aircraft, Heinkels and Messerschmidts, were shot down on the Selsey peninsula, and the first bombs were dropped on East Beach in August 1940. On 14 September a Heinkel bomber, apparently searching for Portsmouth dockyards, dropped over a dozen 500-pounders on the village. Mr. and Mrs. Homer's house in Hillfield Road was hit and almost completely demolished; fortunately most of the family had been out of the house at the time and even Mr. Homer, who was doing some painting and decorating in the house, escaped unscathed though shaken. Three other houses were badly damaged and two were subsequently pulled down. During this raid the gas and water mains were hit but, within four days, normal services were resumed. Later that month another bomb fell on the beach immediately in front of the *Marine Hotel*. Windows were shattered in many houses in Hillfield Road, Clayton Road and Seal Road, but there was no structural damage and no casualties. Sadly, however, one aged resident, Mr. J. Ayling, died of shock a few days later. The next morning a huge unexploded bomb was found lying within 15 yards of Selsey's main gasometer. The gasworks had to be evacuated and the Royal Engineers and men of the 10th Infantry Brigade made the bomb safe before removing and destroying it. Many hit-and-run air raids occurred during 1940. On 19 August the chalets of Broadreeds holiday camp were hit and three evacuees from the London area were killed, including a 13-year-old crippled boy. They were the only civilians to lose their lives in Selsey during this war[29] though there were 43 civilian casualties. Many villagers had commented on the folly of housing evacuees in Broadreeds as there was an ack-ack battery at the end of Seal Road to the west of the camp and a searchlight battery to the north-east, both natural targets for the Germans. The 300 children in the camp were re-evacuated the following day.

From the end of 1940 troops of the 2nd Canadian Division were stationed at Norton Priory. Land at Church Norton had been used as a private aerodrome in the 1930s and was requisitioned by the R.A.F. in July 1942 in spite of strong opposition from the Ministry of Agriculture. Work by an R.A.F. construction unit began early in 1943, including demolition of barns and outbuildings and the construction of a runway in the form of a cross. Norton Priory, Mitchards Croft and cottages near Cole's Farm were earmarked for accommodation. Squadrons of Spitfires and Typhoons were soon installed at Norton and, later, Belgian and French airmen were stationed there. On 6 June 1944, D-Day, four squadrons of Free French Spitfires flew from Norton, heading for Arramanches in Normandy, returning within 40 minutes to be re-fuelled and re-armed. By March 1945, however, local farmers were given permission to graze sheep and cattle on the land again and the site was de-requisitioned soon after the end of the war. There is now virtually no sign of the existence of this very successful air base. The current owners of Norton Priory are in possession of a certificate presented to Mrs. Marion Holden, wife of Major Norman Holden who owned the house from 1919 to 1947, by Queen Elizabeth in appreciation of her sacrifice in opening the doors of the Priory during the war years 'to strangers who were in need of shelter'. Sadly, this hospitality was sometimes abused. By the time Eric Low-Beer bought Norton Priory in 1947 all but one of its fine muster of peacocks had been slaughtered by Canadian servicemen.

Spring 1941 was a bad time for Selsey. During the night of 9/10 March some two dozen 250 kg. bombs hit the village and incendiaries fell like confetti. Although there was considerable structural damage to buildings and many houses lost their roofs, there were no serious casualties. On 8 April more bombs fell in the Broadreeds area; the raiders were apparently attempting to knock out the anti-aircraft and searchlight batteries there. In September 1942 two bouncing bombs were dropped on Selsey. One knocked a chimney off the *Marine Hotel* and damaged the U.S. sailors' quarters, injuring 30 servicemen. Bombing continued almost to the end. On 24 April 1944, 24 bombs were dropped on Selsey or the surrounding sea. Miraculously, there were no casualties but many houses, especially in Seal Road, had to be evacuated and their residents accommodated in a local rest centre. In all, 1,090 buildings in Selsey are said to have been damaged by enemy action during the Second World War.

Then in June 1944 the Allied forces landed in Normandy and there was no further risk of a German attack on the Sussex coast. Before D-Day the assault forces required every inch of room in the Solent area. Selsey was converted into a minor naval base as the Mulberry

72. Troops taking wood out across the hastily-constructed walkway to the emergency landing pier being built out at sea. In the background are the Phoenix caissons or floating concrete harbours which were to be laid on the sea bed off the coast of Normandy so that vehicles could drive straight off the ships onto the 'Mulberry Harbour' as it was known and onto the French beaches. This work took place in the deep-water channel near the end of Park Lane between January and June 1940.

Harbour was prepared for the Normandy landings and, according to *The Daily Sketch* in October 1944, 'looked as if someone had picked up Chicago and put it down on the Sussex foreshore' (*see* illustration 72). The end of the war saw the removal of the emergency batteries, the destruction of defence works and the gradual restoration of beaches for public use and pleasure.

73. Armistice Day at the war memorial, *c.*1951. Rev. Handisyde is conducting the service and Air Vice Marshal Langford-Sainsbury (with his back to the church) was leading the parade of the British Legion.

During the Second World War the Selsey lifeboat station was extremely busy, launching a total of 50 times, 38 calls coming as a result of crashed, or reported crashed, aeroplanes. On most occasions the lifeboatmen found only wreckage or patches of oil, but they did save a number of airmen. In July 1940, for example, they picked up Squadron Leader J. R. A. Peel, whose plane had been shot down by a German, 3½ miles south-west of Selsey. He was taken to Tangmere by ambulance but was back in the air the following day. He later wrote to the coxswain, 'When you arrived I had given up hope of being picked up alive and I doubt whether I would have lasted more than a few minutes. Your skill in finding me in that rough sea seems a miracle to me, and goes to prove that you and all your fellows in the Lifeboat Service are doing a magnificent job of work.'[30] In August of the same year the coastguard reported that two aircraft had crashed five miles south-west of his lookout, so the *Canadian Pacific II* was quickly launched. The lifeboatmen found two wounded German airmen in the water, picked them up and handed them over to the military authorities once back on land. The year 1940 proved to be the busiest yet known for the Selsey lifeboat. She was called out 26 times, on all but two occasions to crashed aircraft.

Tragically, 48 more names were added to the base of the war memorial in St Peter's churchyard, commemorating local men killed in action between 1939 and 1945. These included many young men remembered also on stones in Norton churchyard, such as Sgt. Albert Pennycord, R.A.F., 'Reported missing 8 April 1943. Aged 23 years'.

Chapter Twelve

Domestic Architecture in Selsey

One of the most typical and charming features of Selsey in the 19th century was its thatched cottages, some of great antiquity. Sadly, many were pulled down during redevelopment earlier in the present century and can be appreciated today only through old photographs. Many of these cottages had thatched roofs which extended almost to the ground on the windward side as protection against driving rains, as can be seen in the photographs of Iron Latch Cottage and Ivy Cottage. The demolition of Pennicott's shop (Ladies and Gentlemen's Tailors) in the High Street[31] in the late 1920s, prior to rebuilding, revealed the curious method of house construction used in the 17th century when many of these old cottages were built. The shop, a converted farmhouse of that period, was built without any foundations as we know them today. A base of enormous blocks of stone was laid on the surface of the ground and the walls were built up on these from huge flints and boulders quarried from the Mixon Reef. Almost all the old houses of Selsey were built of beach-gathered flints, knapped into roughly regular shapes. As it is almost impossible to to shape a building's corners or features such as doorways in flint, the Mixon limestone was exploited for this. Some Mixon rock can be collected on the beach as a result of weathering of the reef and until the early 19th century the reef itself was quarried for local use. At that time the Admiralty is said to have forbidden quarrying on the grounds that it was undermining the natural defences of the coast and might lead to a shifting of sand and so become a danger to shipping. In the 1920s, whenever an old house was demolished in Selsey, the Mixon Reef blocks fetched high prices for use as architectural features in new buildings, in walls and rockeries.

Fortunately some attractive old buildings have survived. Just to the south of the church on the west side of the High Street is a long low building with walls of stone rubble (Mixon rock) with brick dressings and quoins and a thatched roof. It probably dates back to the early 17th century, but was extended to the north in 1728 and since then has been much modernised. The brick doorway in front of the north part is inscribed 'P.H. 1728'. This charming building used to be known as the Old Farmhouse but today it is called Sessions Cottage as the Lord of the Manor used to hold his court sessions there. It retains many period features including beams and panelling. Stable Cottage was built in the 18th century and was once the stable block for this court house. It has wooden panelling to all four walls of the dining room, taken from the original looseboxes. Another unusual feature is the thatched and timber granary in the garden dating from the same period, which rests on steddle stones to raise it above damp and vermin.

'The Malt House', nearly opposite at 33 High Street, is another attractive building. Built originally *c.*1571 as a working malthouse and granary, it is constructed of mellow red brick with panels of inset nap flint under a clay tiled roof. The present building has been very much altered and restored. It has an impressive main entrance inset with herringbone brick and inlaid beams, and ornate carving on the upper eaves. Inside was an oak panelled hall and a superb galleried landing and throughout the building were a multitude of exposed beams. The malthouse, described as such as late as 1897 in the Overseers' Rates Book when Lambert Stubington was owner/occupier, used to supply malt to the local breweries and grain to Medmerry Mill. A maltman, Charles Clarke, is described as living in the High Street in the 1851 census. The building was converted into a private house in the 1920s.

74. The Malt House in the 1950s, before its conversion to a nursing home. Note the splendid main entrance.

Mrs. Septimus Ponder, for example, is known to have lived in the house from 1926 until at least the mid-1930s and it was later the home of Major Wills of the tobacco family. It has since been considerably modernised and is now a nursing home.

Tadd's Cottage Gallery is a period property further along the High Street in a conservation area. It is an L-shaped building, the south wing constructed of stone rubble and dating to the 18th century, while the east wing was built of coursed stone and cobbles early in the 19th century. The entire building has a tiled roof. Inside there are stone fireplaces, exposed beams and a fine old bread oven.

'The Homestead', still further south at 154 High Street, on the corner of Knap Lane,[32] is one of the few typical old farmhouses remaining in Selsey. It is a 16th- or 17th-century house of red brick with a hipped thatched roof. It has been almost completely restored with modern brickwork, but in the back wall is an original window with oak diamond-shaped mullions. It has been a private residence for some time and was once the home of Dr. Percy Barford.

There are several more ancient buildings in the High Street, mainly of stone and brick with thatched roofs. These include Iron Latch Cottage (built in the 17th century or even earlier), Century Cottage (an 18th-century house faced with modern rough plaster, and having a thatched roof with three 'eyebrows'), Old Rose Cottage (built of stone rubble with red brick dressings and quoins and with the date *c.*1700 carved over the front door), and Hollyhocks (a 17th-century cottage faced with cobbles and stone rubble, and with brick dressings and quoins; it has a thatched roof with three 'eyebrows'). At one time the High Street was lined with thatched cottages such as these, but relatively few have survived recent commercial development.

North of West Street at 10 Crablands is 'Ivy Cottage', an L-shaped building, the back or south-east wing being a 17th-century timber-framed building with infilling of flints and the

75. Iron Latch Cottage in 1987. Note the thatch extending almost to ground level on the left, north-facing side.

76. 'Hollyhocks' in the High Street in 1930 with Mr. Riddick standing in the garden.

77. Ivy Cottage, Crablands, in 1987.

front or main wing, also 17th-century, built of stone rubble with red brick dressings, quoins and stringcourse. It has a hipped thatched roof. The central chimney stack has wide fireplaces and the open-timbered ceilings have heavy beams and joists.

In Albion Road, near the *Lifeboat Inn*, there used to be a fine large barn which was part of Fish Shop Farm and had nine 10-foot bays with aisles, walls of squared stones and a thatched roof. This barn has been pulled down and the 360 acres which once made up the farm are now down by the sea walls and the land which is not under water is the site of an estate of modern pseudo-Georgian houses. Many other old barns have now been pulled down – there are said to have been 17 barns on the peninsula at one time. These included Woolhouse, Oxstall, Boathouse, Penfold and Farringdon barns, all standing within a few miles of Selsey village in 1907. Woolhouse barn was destroyed by a vandal in 1958; he put a match to the thatch and then boasted of his action afterwards. A few ancient barns have survived the ravages of time and modernisation and are now listed buildings. These include an 18th-century stone barn with part thatched and part slated roof at Crablands Farm, and an 18th-century barn at Greenlease Farm which is faced with tarred weather-boarding and has a hipped thatched roof.

Buildings other than thatched cottages and barns deserve a brief mention. Hale Farm, home of the Woodman family, was situated in the High Street and had lime-washed walls

78. A thatched barn typical of those found in profusion on the Selsey peninsula until recently. This particular example, photographed in 1958, stood at Church Norton.

79. Hale Farm, High Street, *c.*1903: the thatched farm buildings. The message, written on the back of the postcard by a visitor staying on the farm, refers to Miss Woodman as proprietor.

80. Home Farm House, Norton.

81. High House, West Street, demolished in 1937.

82. Houses at the north end of the High Street, *c.*1903. This view has changed little today except that the thatched waggon shed has been removed to the Weald and Downland Open Air Museum at Singleton, the far house is now an antiques shop, and a pavement has been built in front of the row of houses.

of stone and flint with brick dressings. The east gable end towards the road was inscribed 'TS 1699', proclaiming the builder as Thomas Sheppard of Sidlesham. The house had a distinctive herringbone pattern of roof tiling. By 1937 it had been converted into a boarding house, but in the 1940s part of it was pulled down for road widening and the last part was demolished in 1962. A Shell Garage now occupies the site. The Home Farm House in Norton was a very attractive 17th-century building constructed of brick and flint, later cement rendered, with an interior incorporating a wealth of exposed timbering. This was home to Charles Rusbridge for many years, but was tragically demolished in the late 1950s. Some farmhouses, fortunately, have survived. These include Cole's farmhouse, a fine old early Georgian residence, substantially built in brick and stone, with a tiled roof and a doorway at the head of four steps with Doric pilasters, a triglyph frieze and a pediment. Sadly this house suffered severe damage in the gales of October 1987.

High House in West Street was the home of the Claytons, a family of yeoman farmers. The house had been built in 1716 by a Clayton, though the family had lived on the Bill from a much earlier date. In 1851 a James Clayton was assessed by the Overseers of the Poor to pay 4s. 6d. for his house and £2 12s. 10½d. for the land at High House Farm. In February 1936 a later James Clayton died and by May 1937 *The Chichester Post* was reporting that the house had been pulled down. 'Unwept, unhonoured and unsung, the oldest remaining Georgian house in Selsey village has disappeared under the pickaxes of the house-breakers who have thus short-circuited the work of the marine breakers which have steadily advanced towards its destruction.' When it was first built, High House had been 700 yards from the high-water mark, but by the 1930s it was only 200 yards from the edge of the cliff. The house itself is said to have had no real claim to architectural beauty or distinction, but its demolition represented the disappearance of one of the last relics of Selsey's manorial days.

Bill House, still standing in Grafton Road, was built in 1907 as a private residence by the architect M. H. Baillie Scott in an Arts and Crafts vernacular revival style. The building is pebble-dashed and painted, with exposed stone dressings, some stone and flint chequer work and exposed timber framing to the tower gallery. This tower, with its pyramidal bellcast roof and weather vane, is the most unusual feature of the house and was for many years used as a look-out post by the Selsey coastguards (*see* plate 43). Inside the house some Arts and Crafts-style plasterwork of leaves and grapes survives. Bill House is now a grade II listed building in two acres of gardens leading directly to its own stretch of sea shore. It was converted into a residential home for the elderly in 1985.

More humble homes deserve a mention, too. The row of houses at the top (north) end of the High Street (Nos. 26 to 42), for example, date from the early 19th century. The houses are faced with stone rubble and have red brick dressings and quoins. They have a tiled roof and casement windows. Adjoining them is a small single-storey thatched building faced with cobbles, built in the 18th century. The attics of all these houses are connected and may well have been used by smugglers in the last century.

The old Manor House itself is still standing, though by the early 20th century it had ceased to perform the function its name indicates and was known instead as Manor Farm. It remained as three farm cottages for many years but is today part of the Willows retirement homes in Manor Farm Court, a little to the north of the church and the village. It is now a listed building and probably retains some of the structures erected or enlarged by Bishop Robert Sherburne early in the 16th century. However, it has undergone many changes and it is impossible to trace the original plan of the house. It is a rectangular building facing west, the front faced with squared rubble of Mixon rock with flint chippings in the joints (said to keep the devil at bay!). It has brick dressings to the windows and the angles, and a brick eaves cornice, all dating to the end of the 17th century. The roof is tiled, though

83. The Manor House around 1909 when the property was being used as a farm. The exterior has changed little since then, though the trees and the lean-to building at the left have disappeared, and the windows on the far right are no longer bow windows.

traces of thatch were discovered in the early 1970s, and the ancient chimney stacks have been rebuilt. South-west of the house there used to be a thatched barn of seven bays with aisles, its walls built of Mixon rock rubble and brick. As recently as 1961 the house in its two acres of gardens was advertised for sale at only £9,750 and at that time was still arranged around the fine inner hall and what was described as a minstrel's gallery on the landing. In fact, this grandiose-sounding feature was simply a small landing overlooking the stairwell and linking two attics. Sadly it has now been demolished, along with much 17th-century oak panelling and open-timbered ceilings, though the superb 17th-century oak staircase at the rear of the house remains. Another interesting feature to have survived the recent restoration work is the fireplace in the right-hand ground floor room which has a beam scratched with three graffiti sailing ships. This beam was rescued from the 17th-century barn which was burnt down around 1972. There is an ancient well behind the house with a fine circular brick shaft.

The Old Rectory, now Norton Priory, is the most interesting and certainly the most ancient building in the parish though it has been altered so often that its development is largely conjectural. For many centuries it was the home of the rectors of Selsey, but it was never a priory as such. The first written record of the Rectory is in 1340 when the rector living there had 16 acres of land valued at 32 shillings a year and one dovecote. In 1672 the Rectory was leased to Sir Henry Peckham, Recorder, of Chichester. Dr. King was then rector and the house was described as 'a decayed little mansion'. Sir Henry almost totally rebuilt the house and in the early 19th century Rev. Barré Phipps added a section to the western end of the building.

Some of the walls of the Rectory contain infill dating back to Roman times and there is Saxon work in some of the foundations. The western portion of the house is medieval. A small 15th-century window was discovered embedded in the south wall of the dining room in 1864 when a new window was being inserted. In the north wall there are two medieval fireplaces adjoining one another, and a third fireplace on the west side seems to suggest that the room may once have been a large refectory. One of the fireplaces was built of Caen stone and is very similar to the tomb of John and Agatha Lewes, possibly even constructed by the same stonemason. Two sets of dated initials were scratched on the lintel: the *Victoria County History* claims these were 'W.I., 1439' and 'A.C., 1489' but today, though the initials are still visible, the first marking looks more like 'W.L., 1539'. The house has been much altered over the centuries. The middle section which faces north and is about 30 feet in length is probably the site of a timber-framed medieval hall, rebuilt with brick and heightened in the late 17th century. Other ancient survivals are a blocked stone doorway at the south end of the west wall of the west wing, a projecting chimney stack of the early 17th century in the west wall of the west wing and, visible externally at the far west of the house, a small original quatrefoil ventilation opening in Caen stone. In 1901 Rev. W. E. Malaher discovered behind the dining room wall two 'cells'. It was suggested at the time that these were punishment cells for monks, but in fact parochial clergy lived in the house, not monks. They could have been secret hiding places during times of religious persecution – the Rectory seems an unlikely hiding place for recusants except that the house was often leased out to wealthy families rather than providing accommodation for the rector. Perhaps the cells were 'tubby holes' for hiding smuggled goods, a plausible explanation in view of the proximity of the house to Pagham Harbour and the fact that there was an underground passage leading from the old kitchen to the churchyard, the roof of which caved in many years ago.

The 38 acres of grounds which surround the house show traces of an ancient shallow moat which existed centuries ago. Earlier in the present century, when violent gales from the south and south-west were accompanied by high tides, the sea used to overflow its banks and often flooded parts of the Rectory grounds. Sea walls were therefore erected in June 1929 at the expense of the owner, Norman Holden. Externally at least, Norton Priory has changed little since the 16th century. Its appearance today is very similar to that portrayed by Bernardi in his picture which now hangs in Chichester Cathedral (*see* page 13).

In 1902/3 Mr. Claude Bishop bought the house from the Rev. John Cavis-Brown and the mortgagees of the property, the Governors of the Bounty of Queen Anne for the Augmentation of the Maintenance of the Poor Clergy, for £2,000. (Rev. W. E. Malaher was the last vicar to have lived in the Old Rectory.) Mr. Bishop improved part of the interior with oak panelling and changed the name of the property from the Rectory to Norton Priory. Some years later it was bought by Mrs. Stephanie Agnes Levita who carried out a great deal of rebuilding and alteration, including the dining room and main bedroom above, which constitute the south wing. Major Norman Holden was owner from 1919 onwards and in 1947 it was bought by Mr. Eric Low-Beer. Norton Priory has been a Grade II listed building

84. The back of Norton Priory, *c.*1909: the entrance porch has now been moved further right and the wing on the extreme right has been brought forward into the lawn (where the basket chair stands in the picture). The two main gables on the left are unchanged.

since 1958 and has now been converted into a luxury retirement home which opened in January 1988.

It is tragic to think that so many houses and barns of architectural importance in Selsey have disappeared to make way for wider roads and modern housing estates. However, there is much of great interest which remains and, for that, all who are interested in the past must be grateful and also willing to fight for the continuing conservation of this unique part of our national heritage.

Chapter Thirteen

Business and Pleasure

Selsey has been a bustling, industrious village from the earliest times. Many people earned their living in occupations related to the sea and these have been considered in earlier chapters. However, there were many other thriving trades and businesses.

There has been a mill in Selsey for many centuries. Today Selsey Mill, often called Medmerry Mill, is a prominent feature of the West Sands Leisure Centre and the ground floor is used for selling holiday souvenirs. There have been mills on or near the same site, at the end of Mill Lane, for well over 300 years, though in the 17th century the mill would have been tidal, with a large pond with flood gates at each end. At high tide the western gate would be closed and the other opened, so that the water flowed through the mill and out into the sea on the east. When this structure disappeared under the waves around the middle of the 18th century, a windmill took its place, further inland and well above the high-water mark. It was a timber building, with a brick and tiled mill house next to it, and took the full force of the elements, so around 1820 it was replaced by a tower windmill built of locally-made red bricks. This tower is still standing today though it is now about 200 yards nearer the tideline than when it was first built. The new building had a white beehive cap around which was built a gallery, the only example of its kind in Sussex, to give the miller easy access when furling or unfurling the four canvas rigged sails or sweeps. These drove two pairs of stones which ground wheat. The mill was also the centre of a salt industry and by 1827 four wrought-iron salt pans, each 9 ft. square, had been installed at a cost of £100.

In October 1828 the entire property was seized under distraint for arrears of rent and put up for sale by auction. The sale embraced not only the windmill itself, all the utensils associated with milling and several lots of household furniture, but also 21 acres of excellent meadow and pasture land. Fortunately the windmill remained intact and was subsequently tenanted and worked by a number of millers and maltsters, including Thomas Faith (miller at Medmerry in the 1841 census), H. R. Arnell (1858-78), Sampson Copestake, and F. W. Sharpe (1882-90). The mill was taken over by Farne and Co. in about 1905, after it had fallen into disrepair. Flour was milled in Selsey until 1910 after which the windmill stood idle for a short time before Holloways of Shoreham were brought in to modernise it. A new windshaft, new sails and gears were fitted, and the gallery and cap rebuilt. The old machinery was replaced with the most up-to-date equipment then available for cracking beans and rolling oats. The work was completed by 1913 but, due to restrictive working conditions imposed during the First World War and the death of the owner, the new venture never really got off the ground. Medmerry Farm, along with the four-bedroomed Mill House and the windmill, were sold by auction in July 1917. The property included 185 acres of 'valuable marshland' which, with the two buildings, was estimated to be worth £250 p.a. Medmerry Mill finished its working life grinding pepper for Farne and Co. in the 1920s.

It then fell into disuse and by 1936 both fan and sails had gone and, when the West Sands site was bought by the White Horse Caravan Company in 1959, the windmill was in a very dilapidated state. Fortunately, Mr. John Bunn, Managing Director of the Caravan Campany, had spent his childhood in Selsey and loved the windmill. So, in addition to developing the caravan site, he decided to restore the mill which was not only a local

85. Medmerry windmill in 1935 – still very much part of a farm, rather than a haven for holiday makers.

landmark but figured on Admiralty charts as a guide for seafarers using the Channel. With the aid of old photographs and advised by the Society for the Protection of Ancient Buildings, a programme of restoration was undertaken. Dummy sweeps were set up and another new cap fitted, into which were inserted large observation windows occupying the whole of the seaward side. This expensive work was completed in 1961. Weather damage made it necessary to remove the dummy sails, but a new set was fitted in 1977 and the whole four-storey mill is today in splendid condition, a permanent reminder of the generations of millers who lived and worked in Selsey.

In a small village like Selsey all the inhabitants were dependent on each other in many ways. No man could work in isolation and this can be demonstrated using names taken from *Kelly's Directory* for the early years of this century. The miller could not operate unless his mill was in good repair, so he would need to call on the services of a builder, Alfred John Cutler, or Henry Arnell Smith, who was also a brickmaker. There were several brickfields in Selsey during the 19th century and in the early years of the present century: one near Ferry (Selsey Multi Stock Brick Co. Ltd.), one by the British Legion building in the field behind the Malt House, and one by the tram line in Chichester Road near to the site of the modern police houses. This was the Trojan Manufacturing Co. Ltd. which closed

86. Men at work on Manor Farm in about 1917. The photograph was probably taken in a field south of Drift Road and Charlie Wakely is driving the tractor.

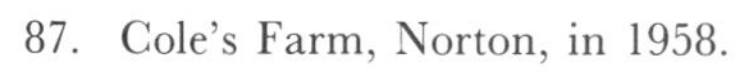

87. Cole's Farm, Norton, in 1958.

around 1930 because the clay seam began to peter out and because of the general economic depression.

In the same way the miller would have no work unless there was grain to grind, so he was totally dependent on the farmers in the area. In 1909 these included Aaron Bailey at Greenlees (sometimes Greenlease) Farm in Norton, James Clayton at High House, and William North at Ferry House. The 1841 census records 18 farmers (presumably *owners* of land) and 67 agricultural labourers, so in the mid-19th century the land was still the largest employer of labour. The 1851 and later censuses give more details of farmers. Some owned only small farms. John Summers of the High Street, for example, farmed 70 acres and employed four labourers, whereas Hugh Penfold farmed 380 acres at Norton, giving occupation to 14 labourers. The normal working life span in the 19th century was considerably longer than it is today – in 1841 John Osborn was recorded as an agricultural labourer at the age of 80 and at the other end of the scale George Shepherd was recorded as farmer's boy (as opposed to 'scholar') in the 1851 census, at the tender age of nine years. Similarly, Alfred James, also nine, was classified as a plough boy in 1861. Other very young children worked as carter boys and cow boys. Details of some Selsey farms can be found in sales particulars lodged in the County Record Office. In May 1872, for example, three farms were sold by auction after the death of the Hon. Mrs. Vernon-Harcourt. These were Home Farm with its 144 acres of highly productive arable, meadow and pasture land, let to William Cosens Woodman at a rent of £220 p.a., Cole's Farm with 275 acres leased to Hugh Penfold at £261 p.a., and the Manor Farm with 640 acres of land extending from the

88. Sheep shearers stop work to pose for a photograph in a barn in Selsey High Street. In 1872 Messrs. William and Lambert Stubington of Manor Farm sold by auction a flock of Southdown sheep which they had bred. The ewes fetched from 55s. to 90s. per head and the wether lambs fetched between 30s. 6d. and 47s. per head, all good prices for that time.

89. Ellis & Sons provisions store in the High Street, *c.*1937. William Charles Ellis is standing on the left, with William Hollingdale next to him, then Winifred Sluman, apprentice Ron Mant, Beryl Sparshott, and on the far right, Clifton 'Boy' Ellis. The two girls sat at the large desk just inside the shop and acted as cashiers, one for the grocer's and one for the butcher's department.

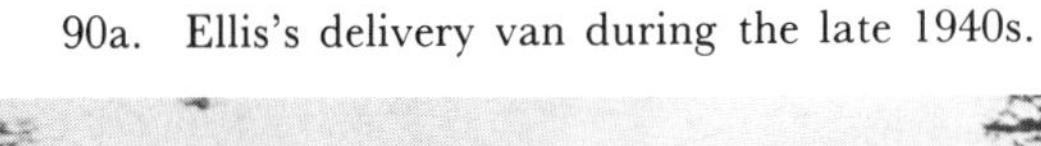

90a. Ellis's delivery van during the late 1940s.

Manor House right down to the Bill and let to William Stubington at £640 p.a. All these farms had thatched granaries built on stone pillars.

One Selsey farmer at least gained a worldwide reputation. This was Hugh Penfold whose Southdown ram, no. 121, was exported to America after the Chichester sale in June 1892. The following November *The West Sussex Gazette* reported that it had won seven first prizes as well as four championships, against rams of all ages and breeds. The Manor Farm flock of Southdown sheep belonging to the Pagham Harbour Company and managed by Mr. Newton Clayton was well known nationwide around the turn of the century, taking a prominent position in all the leading agricultural shows in England. At a sale in Selsey in August 1903, ewes and rams from this flock were bought by farmers the length and breadth of the country and fetched very high prices. One yearling ram alone fetched 21 guineas and the sale realised a total of £2,050.

Telephone 5 Selsey

Ellis & Sons

Family Grocers, Bakers, Confectioners & Butchers

Wines & Spirits. Ale & Stout Merchants

Specialities:

Home-killed Meat. Home-made Bread
Wedding, Christening & Fancy Cakes

HIGH STREET
SELSEY - ON - SEA

90b. An advertisement for Ellis & Sons, *c.*1930.

Having received grain from the farmers, the miller would produce flour which would be supplied to the local bakers such as Mrs. Rosena Wingham who had a bakehouse in one of the thatched cottages in the High Street (later demolished to make way for the cinema hall) in the early years of this century. The Selsey peninsula, with its fertile medium loam, still possesses some of the finest corn-growing land in the south of England. Diversification has taken place, however, and Selsey farms now breed cattle or grow market-garden crops as well as grain. When Home Farm came up for sale in 1956 its fine herd of 140 purebred attested dairy cattle was given prominence in the advertisement.

The farmers would also have supplied the local butchers, and the grocers and provisions dealers, such as William Charles Ellis (1870-1961). He married Mary Ellen Petts and their fathers founded the company known as Ellis and Petts around 1890, trading from a shop opposite the Bible Christian chapel until about 1904. In that year the business moved further down the High Street to the Croat, where Homes and Gardens have their shop today. These premises, Nos. 132-138 High Street, had been leased in 1731 by Henry Binstead of Chichester to Henry Warner of Selsey for the sum of five shillings. Henry Warner was a distant ancestor of the Ellis family. The shop continued as Ellis and Sons from about 1918: three sons, Ray, Guy and Clifton, were all actively involved in the business. Many older residents of Selsey will remember Ellis's for the sight and smell of its fresh-baked bread and cakes, ground coffee, cheese, and bacon flitches hanging from the ceiling. Everything in the shop was scrupulously clean, the shelves packed to capacity and the assistants were invariably friendly and had time for a chat with customers. Mr. Hart made a daily delivery of bread from Ellis's bakehouse on his horse and cart and, in the shop's hey-day, four boys made deliveries of general provisions, piled into wicker baskets on the front of their bicycles. It was a sad day for Selsey when Ellis's ceased trading in June 1972. Ellis's would have received supplies from dairymen such as Edward Arnell and Walter Jinman, as well as from the farmers and bakers.

Many people in a small village used to follow several trades. Alfred Woodland (1845-1914) was sub postmaster at Selsey in 1899. The post office was in the High Street (though

91. Edward Arnell's milk delivery cart in the High Street, *c.*1912.

the original village post office was at Rose Cottage, an 18th-century thatched building in Rectory Lane, Church Norton) and from these premises he also acted as draper and wine and spirit merchant. A new post office in the High Street was opened in 1914 opposite where Tadd's Gallery stands today. Henry Arnell Smith, already described as builder and brickmaker, was also the village decorator and undertaker. James Sherrington was both bootmaker and carrier, and Stephen Jenman was both confectioner and hairdresser from premises in the High Street.

Selsey seems to have had men following almost all the essential trades at the turn of the century – as well as those mentioned above, the village could boast a coal merchant, a draper, a milliner, a wheelwright, stationers and newsagents. Selsey Drapery Bazaar was owned by John Ewen Thomas Ayling who moved to the village in 1892. In 1901 he bought a cottage in the High Street and opened his drapery, selling a wide variety of goods, ranging from pins, elastic and ribbon to curtains, ladies' hats and men's shirts. This family-run business continued until 1912. The early 19th-century building is today occupied by Coffin's electrical shop.

Selsey's coal merchant was Edward George Arnell, born in the mid-19th century, and later chairman of Chichester R.D.C. and alderman of the West Sussex County Council. He began his working life as a fisherman. He also sold locally-caught fish which had to be hauled to Chichester station by horses in those days. To keep the horses working during the winter when little fishing was possible, Mr. Arnell began a small coal business. Coal was

92a. Woodland's Stores, which included a sub-post office, *c.*1909.

92b. An advertisement for Woodland's Stores, *c.*1909.

Try our Special Blended Tea at 1/6 per lb.

A. WOODLAND,

Butcher, - Grocer, - Draper.

Purveyor of English Meat only.

WINE, SPIRIT AND BEER MERCHANT.

(Agent for GILBEY'S).

Fruit and Vegetables fresh daily.

Post Office Stores, High Street,

- Selsey. -

93. The later post office in the High Street (between the two sets of trees on the left). This card was postmarked 1917.

94. Selsey Drapery Bazaar in the High Street: a postcard sent in 1909.

brought to Selsey by sea in small colliers which were beached at low tide and had to be unloaded before high tide. Some 50 tons were unloaded in a tide and men received 2d. per ton for the work. Arnell's advertisements claim that his coal business was established in 1886. Arnell was a pillar of the local establishment. As well as being closely involved with local government, he was Governor of the Chichester High Schools for both boys and girls, Chairman of the Selsey branch of the National Lifeboat Institution, President of the Selsey branch of the Conservative Association and, from 1914, a J.P. for Sussex.

Coal Fires for Health, Comfort and Economy.

Make your Homes bright & cheerful for XMAS

By getting your Fuel from—
E. G. ARNELL & SON
The Old Established Firm

Specialities :

BEST DINING and DRAWING ROOM COAL
Very Hot and Clean.

BEST KITCHEN
A good Coal for all Household Purposes.

ANTHRACITE BOILER NUTS — MACHINE MADE COKE NUTS
For all Furnaces and closed Stoves—Highly Recommended.

Sole Agents for COALITE the "Smokeless" Fuel."

Well seasoned Oak and Beech Logs at per load or per ton.

Special quotations for large or small quantities on application to—

E. G. ARNELL & SON,

Coal Merchants : **HIGH STREET, SELSEY**
Established 1886 Phone Selsey 8
Free delivery within a radius of 10 miles.

95. E. G. Arnell, Coal Merchant: an advertisement issued at Christmas 1931.

No community would be complete without its publicans, of course. In the 1890s there seem to have been four public houses in Selsey. James Mitchell was landlord of the *Crown Inn*, which is believed to have been an inn as early as the 16th century, though the present building was erected in the 18th century. In 1979 workmen on the premises in the High Street came across an 18 ft. deep well which may perhaps have been the village well in Elizabethan times. The *Crown* was often used as the venue for auctions in the 19th and early 20th centuries. Walter Arnell Smith (1863-1915) was landlord of the *Fisherman's Joy* on the corner of East Street and Manor Road. The *Albion* was built around 1800, but in 1970 was renamed the *Lifeboat Inn*. William Brooks was landlord in the 1890s. Finally, there was the *New Inn*, almost opposite the *Crown*. The *New Inn* claims to have been established in 1856 but was known as the *Neptune* by the 1930s. The building dates to the 18th century and was often used for inquests, especially after deaths by drowning at sea. In the 1890s many of

96. The *Crown Inn*, *c*.1904. The notice on the right of the building advertises the stables. Note the absence of the Pavilion (cinema) to the left of the public house.

97. The *Albion Inn* (now the *Lifeboat*) around 1910 when James Ray was landlord.

98. Male's Forge in the 1920s, with Thomas Male on the left, his brother on the right and Toby Lee in the doorway. The board by the side of the door displayed the Selsey tramway's timetable.

99. Gates given to the Selsey boy scouts (the company was founded in 1950) in memory of Thomas Male, blacksmith, who died in 1972.

Selsey's public houses were owned by Henty & Sons Ltd., though James Northeast of the *New Inn* advertised in *The West Sussex Gazette* throughout that decade as 'an agent for G. S. Constable's celebrated Littlehampton ales and stout, supplied in 4½, 6, 9 and 18 gallon casks, from 10d. a gallon. Also in Imperial Pints, screw-stoppered bottles, at 2s. 6d. to 3s. per dozen.' By the 1920s the two firms seem to have amalgamated and become Henty & Constable. By 1909 Joseph Davis is recorded as proprietor at the *Selsey Hotel* and by 1918 Harry Meakin was advertising the good bathing, tennis and fishing at the *Marine Hotel*. A few details are available to bring this catalogue of names to life. In 1914 *The Chichester Observer* ran a story entitled 'Weak Brandy at Selsey'. Alfred George Mitchell, landlord of the *Crown*, had been summoned for selling brandy 'not of the nature, substance and quality demanded'. Under analysis it was found to be 33.1 under proof – water must have been added to the extent of almost 11 per cent. Mr. Mitchell could not explain this and said that to his knowledge water had never been added to the alcohol he sold. He was fined £5 and asked to pay costs of £1 7s.

There was no ancient iron industry in Selsey, though Sussex was important from an early date for its smelting furnaces. However, there were three blacksmiths recorded in the 1841 census: Charles Prior, Charles Voke and Cornelius Steer. In 1904 George Male, a Westcountryman who executed work of artistic excellence in iron, took over a property in West Street as a forge. The tiled building, which became known as 'Sea Star' from a ship's sign washed ashore and fitted to the front of the forge, dated back to the late 18th century but has sadly now been pulled down. At the start of the present century there were some 200 horses in Selsey belonging to local farmers and tradesmen. Shoeing these, repairing carts and farm machinery, and manufacturing ornamental ironwork kept George Male fully occupied. By 1934 Thomas Male and Courtney were advertising as blacksmiths in West Street. Magnificent gates can now be seen in School Lane made from old tools and machinery parts (bolt cutters, spanners, pliers, shears, pilhooks, nails, and also horseshoes and traps) from the Sea Star Forge in West Street. They were given to the Selsey boy scouts in memory of the late Thomas Male, 'blacksmith and farrier, 1910-72'. Even today B. J. Male & Son, blacksmiths and engineers, work from premises in West Street, on welding, steel fabrications, wrought ironwork, and repairing garden tools. Male's is the oldest established business surviving in Selsey. New houses further down West Street, on the site of the old works, have been named 'The Forge'.

100. A Pullinger mouse trap.

A most unusual trade was pursued by Colin Pullinger, born at Ivy Cottage in 1815. Pullinger is described in early directories as 'inventive manufacturer'. The invention for which he is chiefly remembered is a mousetrap, though his trade card describes him as inventor of an improved horse hoe, an improved scarifier, a machine to tar ropes, as well as traps for mice, rats and moles. At one time there was a considerable mousetrap industry in Selsey, with thousands of the contraptions being made and sold every year. By the time of the 1861 census Pullinger is recorded as employing many young boys as mousetrap makers, for example William Morris aged 11 and Samuel Prior aged 12. The trap was most effective – self-setting, it caught the mice alive, could hold more than a dozen and did not inflict any injury on the animals. A door could be opened from the outside and the mice could be dropped over a bucket of water and drowned. Pullinger's mousetrap went on show at the Great Exhibition in 1851 and was said to have fascinated Queen Victoria. The traps were made of beech wood from the Goodwood estate and it took Mr. Pullinger only three minutes to put one together once the materials (nails, wire and wood) had been prepared. The factory was in the High Street, on the site of the parish hall, and at one time employed 40 men and boys for whom Mr. Pullinger supplied a magnificent feast each year on Christmas Eve. In 1883 Mr. Pullinger turned out 960 traps every week. A mouse trap cost 2s. 6d., a rat trap 5s., but for a mere shilling beetles and cockroaches could be caught in one of the famous Pullinger traps. The growing popularity of the penny trap doomed Pullinger's enterprise, for he stated: 'My trap cannot be sold for less than half-a-crown. Still, it is cheap at the price, for it will last a life time.' Colin Pullinger died in 1910 and the business dwindled from a flourishing concern to a one-man enterprise. By the 1920s, Charles Pullinger, grandson of the inventor, was working alone in one small shed, still called 'the factory', but by the 1930s even this had gone, and not a single trap could be bought in Selsey – a sad end to the industry partly responsible for bringing a tramline to the village.

Banking services grew up to cope with the increase of trade and business in the village. The first banks appeared in Selsey at the very start of the 20th century. They were the London and County Bank established in September 1901 as a sub-branch to Chichester, with Edward Wallace as manager and opening only on Fridays from 11 a.m. to 2 p.m., and Barclays, also a sub-branch to Chichester, with the same opening hours and Mr. C. R. Steedon as manager. In those early days the London and County premises were just north of the present Lloyds Bank and the Barclays building was a tiny one in the High Street, almost immediately opposite the present branch. At that time there would have been only two employees in each bank. In 1909 the Westminster Bank took over the London and County branch and by 1934 both Barclays and Westminster had extended their opening hours. Barclays, for example, did business between 10.15 a.m. and 1.45 p.m. on Monday, Tuesday, Thursday and Friday in July, August and September, and on Monday, Wednesday and Friday during the rest of the year. When Barclays moved to its present much larger premises, some time before 1930, they at first used only the ground floor, the top floor being occupied by the village's veterinary surgeon.

These early banks were joined by Lloyds in 1946, again a sub-branch to Chichester, with just a cashier and guard. In September 1965 it became an independent branch and by 1969 it had severed all links with Chichester, and Mr. Jeff Donnely was manager. Today there are six full-time employees and a part-time typist. The other banks expanded in the same way. The Westminster Bank became an independent sub-branch in 1946 and a full branch in 1961. Barclays was granted full branch status in 1936 and is now the largest bank in Selsey, employing nine full-time members of staff. In 1986 the Barclays premises were designated a grade II listed building of great architectural importance within the Selsey village conservation area. The red brick building dates to the 18th century, though it has been much altered and restored since then.

Many other changes have taken place in the village within recent years, such as the building of a new shopping precinct on the corner of the High Street and West Street in the early 1970s. Many of the old shops, like Ellis's, have disappeared, to be replaced by the uniform and characterless buildings which supply the needs of the modern village.

Not everyone in Selsey was prosperous of course. There was little unemployment in the village in the 19th century but some poverty existed especially among the elderly. In 1861, for instance, Mary Tadd aged 72 was recorded as receiving parish relief, as was Charlotte

101. The High Street premises which originally housed Barclays Bank. The tiny building almost opposite the present bank stood next to Meade's Star Tea Company and later became Simpson's hairdresser's; a second storey was built on top to provide living accommodation (*see* illustration 57a).

102. Barclays Bank in the 1980s, now a grade II listed building.

Farrow aged 77 who had earlier in life supported herself as a charwoman. Sixty-four-year-old Anne Beale was described as a pauper in the same census return. It was not only elderly women who were supported by the parish in the days before state pensions – in 1871 William Willshire, aged 71, who had been an agricultural labourer but was now presumably unable to work, depended on parish relief. Those who could afford to do so made subscriptions to Friendly Societies to safeguard themselves against hard times. The most important self-help group in the village was the 'Star of Selsey', part of the Court of Foresters. In 1904 this group had 267 adult members and 15 juniors. It had assets of over £3,700 and in the previous year had paid out £157 11s. 8d. in sick pay and £24 for funeral expenses. The Foresters seem to have made a profit most years, apparently because claims for sickness payments were low and rates of interest paid on money invested were good, averaging 3½ per cent!

For the most part, the land and the sea have provided the people of Selsey with a comfortable living and the villagers have shown initiative and enterprise in building up small businesses to meet the multifarious needs of the community.

The people of Selsey could never be accused of 'all work and no play'. From the earliest days the village has been a close-knit community, residents enjoying their leisure time together after a hard working day. Much home-spun entertainment would have been available in the public houses (*see* page 129) and as early as 1885 a public hall was opened in the village, now the British Legion hall in the High Street. There was one large room with a permanent stage at one end and seating space for 250, as well as several ante rooms. In October of 1885 a Mr. Fred Lockyer gave an evening's entertainment of magical illusions, musical selections and ventriloquism to a large audience to test the acoustics of the new building. A few weeks later the hall was formally opened by the President of the Chichester Division of the Liberal Association at the inaugural meeting of Selsey's Liberal Club.

The Liberals did not have the monopoly of this hall. In 1890 Lord Walter Gordon-Lennox, Conservative M.P. for West Sussex, addressed a large gathering there on political affairs and in April 1891 the Primrose League held a meeting there, Gordon-Lennox presiding. In his speech he said that a general election was expected soon and called upon members of the league to try to influence the Radicals in Selsey, believed to outnumber the Conservatives at this date. In June 1892 Gordon-Lennox offered himself as candidate to represent the Chichester division of Sussex in Parliament. He pledged his support for Lord Salisbury's government (1886-92) which, he said, had an excellent record, having maintained peace, restored order to Ireland and passed several acts to promote the interests of the labouring classes. He denounced Gladstone's Liberal policies, particularly his support for Home Rule in Ireland, and concluded by stating, 'I shall always endeavour to further your local interests to the best of my ability'. The election finally took place in July 1892. Selsey voters could choose between Gordon-Lennox and Mr. Herbert Reid, the Liberal candidate. The local result was announced in Chichester on 13 July, Gordon-Lennox winning by a majority of 1,875. So, Selsey continued to be represented in parliament by a Conservative M.P., though Gladstone and the Liberals formed the new national government.

A second building for public entertainments was opened in 1913 – the Pavilion or cinema in the High Street. Built by Mr. Hocking, it could seat about 350 people, at first on fold-away chairs. By the mid-1920s Mr. F. W. Phipps was proprietor and he applied for permission to give cinema performances on Sundays, claiming that this would be of value to the village as its population had increased by 1,500 over the previous two to three years. The Chichester magistrates made no objection, believing that Sunday films would help keep young people off the streets. In August 1926, however, just after the building had been emptied following a dance, a disastrous fire broke out in the cinema hall, causing £2,000

103a. The Pavilion in the High Street in the 1920s, with posters advertising the latest films. The cinema hall was built on the site of an old thatched house.

103b. Pavilion programme for May 1941. At this time there were three changes of programme a week – quite an achievement.

SUNDAY, May 25th.
BORIS KARLOFF and
MARJORIE REYNOLDS in
MR. WONG in CHINATOWN
Also CHASING TROUBLE

MONDAY, May 26th. For 3 Days
PENNY SINGLETON and
ARTHUR LAKE in
BLONDIE ON A BUDGET
Also KONGA

THURSDAY, May 29th. For 3 Days
BORIS KARLOFF and
MARJORIE REYNOLDS in
THE MYSTERY OF THE WENTWORTH CASTLE
Also HEROES IN BLUE

SUNDAY, June 1st.
WALLACE BEERY and
LARAINE DAY in
SERGEANT MADDEN
Also THE KID FROM TEXAS

PAVILION
SELSEY
TELEPHONE 309

PROGRAMME
for MAY, 1941

POPULAR PRICES.
PLEASE KEEP THIS PROGRAMME
:: :: FOR REFERENCE :: ::
NOTE CHANGE OF
OPENING TIMES :
Evening Performance 6-15 p.m.
Saturday Matinee 1-45 p.m.

worth of damage. The back portion of the hall, including the stage and dressing rooms, was saved but the front was badly damaged and the managerial offices gutted. The cinema was out of commission for many months, and sorely missed by residents and holidaymakers alike as not only did it show films, but vaudeville shows and dances were also held in the hall. In September 1925, for example, the Russian Ballet Company (*Théâtre Choreographique*) visited Selsey for one night, performing at the Pavilion. Sophie Tucker often performed there, the unusually high fee of 7s. 6d. being charged for admission to her shows, and the Selsey Follies were regular visitors in the inter-war period. Dan Denton and his group of singers, musicians, dancers and comedians from London at first gave concert parties in a tent with a wooden floor on the sea front. They later performed both in the Pavilion and at the church hall, completely changing their programme every Monday, Wednesday and Friday, admission prices ranging from 6d. to 2s. 4d. The Pavilion continued to operate until the 1960s, though in the later years it showed films only during the summer months and was used for performances of the village pantomime in the winter. The last films were shown around 1957.

Sporting activities have always featured prominently in the life of the village. In the early years of the century there was a regatta every August, followed by a carnival procession. So popular was this event that special transport arrangements were made to

104. Crowds enjoying the Selsey Regatta in 1913, with the lifeboat *Lucy Newbon* up on the beach.

105. Children's sports early in this century: these were held every August in the recreation ground in New Road.

106. Children enjoying tea after the sports.

bring in visitors from Bognor and Chichester. There would be a variety of sailing, sculling, dinghy and swimming races, and a water polo match, local people donating the prizes. In fact there was a regatta in Selsey as early as September 1874. That opened with a two-mile galley race between 11 fishermen and 22 members of the Selsey cricket club. This was followed by a punt race, a tub race, a 400-yards swimming race, and finally walking a greasy pole with a leg of mutton at the end. The day was rounded off with a display of rockets and fireworks in the evening. About 70 people participated in the carnival in August 1913 in fancy dress costume, and decorated cars and other vehicles joined the procession which started from Station Road. Villagers and summer visitors lined the streets to watch the colourful parade. In the 1920s there were awards for decorated cars, horse-drawn vehicles, bicycles, perambulators and even houses, and for the best ladies', gentlemen's and children's costumes.

Another annual tradition early in the century was the sports day, also held in August. This took place in the recreation ground in New Road (Hillfield Road), 6d. being charged for admission in 1910, though Selsey schoolchildren were admitted free of charge. A concert was normally given on the same evening in the recreation ground, though the public hall would have been used in case of rain. Queen Victoria's Diamond Jubilee was the cause of great celebrations on 22 June 1897. A 'meat tea' was provided for all people over 50 years of age and a bonfire was lit on the Bill in the evening, accompanied by a display of fireworks. Two days later tea and sports were laid on for all children under 15 and boys over 16 took part in a special sports competition. Neither the annual sports nor the regatta were held during the war years, but the traditions were revived in 1921. Nowadays Selsey carnival takes place in the week leading up to the August Bank Holiday and attracts thousands of participants and spectators, both residents and visitors. In 1987 the carnival raised a splendid £3,700 which was donated to 31 charitable organisations from Selsey and Sidlesham.

There has been a football club in Selsey since at least the start of the present century, probably 1903. In the early days the ground was in the field behind the station building. In 1909 the club won the Chichester and District League championship, but during the First World War it was dissolved as there were so few young men left in the village. After the war another club was started, Selsey Rovers, but organisation was sadly lacking – the players even had to carry the goal posts around with them as they never knew where they would be playing! Eventually Selsey Rovers merged with Selsey F.C. and the situation improved. For one season Selsey had the formidable Bombardier Billy Wells on its books. He was a boxer with a training camp at Selsey, renowned for his fists rather than his feet. His main claim to fame is as the muscular man who hit the gong at the start of Rank films. The club closed again during the Second World War but managed to start up again after the war in spite of financial difficulties. Selsey then tried two seasons in the West Sussex League without any success, so returned to the Chichester and District League. In 1954 the team joined the West Sussex League again and this proved the turning point in its fortunes. In the seven seasons after 1954 they were champions of Division One of the League five times, but four times turned down the chance of playing in a higher class of football because of the travelling expenses involved – most County clubs were in East Sussex. By 1960, however, the club had a fine new £1,500 pavilion and the lease of their pitch, which only needed lengthening to come up to County League specifications. So the team finally took the plunge and was accepted into membership of the County League. In 1987 Selsey was top of Division Two of the Sussex County Football League for much of the season and finally won the Division Two cup, beating Ferring 3-2 in the final. The team is now back in Division One for the first time in 11 years, and members play with all the enthusiasm shown by the earliest players at the start of the century.

107. Selsey football team, winners of the Chichester and District League Cup in the 1927-8 season. The players are: (*back row, left to right*) Wilf Lawrence, Tom Mariner, Rupert Gardner, Ralph Selsby; (*middle row, left to right*) Alf Mant, Len Lawrence, Bill Hart (with the ball), Phil Lawrence, Freddie Head; Seated at the front, Harold 'Doug' Wilmer (*left*) and Harold Smith (*right*). The officials and supporters at the back are (*left to right*): Mr. Dennis, Mr. Tadd, Roly Humphry, George Edwards, Mr. E. G. Arnell (President) and Leo DeLaney. Front left is Roy Langford.

The recreation ground behind the fire station is home to both the football club and the cricket club today and in 1977 Selsey succeeded in getting a cricket pavilion erected on the ground. Selsey has a very long and honourable cricketing tradition. As early as 1834 matches against Chichester, played at Selsey, Goodwood or Kingley Vale, were recorded in local newspapers. The earliest known cricket club played at a ground in Beacon House from the late 1860s until 1879, 'a pleasant place adjoining the sea at Selsey Bill' (*West Sussex Gazette*, 1878), but folded up due to a shortage of local men willing to play in matches. This was not always the case – in July 1869 there were at least 22 local men willing to play in a match at Selsey cricket ground between an eleven from the Factory (presumably Pullinger's) and an eleven from Norton. The club also played matches against a team of Selsey fishermen. In those days there was even a 'juvenile' team, too. The cricket club was re-formed in 1890 and matches against Priory Park are recorded during the later years of the 19th century. Mr. F. Fogden was Club Secretary at that time. In the early years of the present century a heated debate was reported in *The Bognor Observer* because, when an eleven of residents could not be organised, the Selsey club allowed visitors to play in the team, feeling that this was preferable to scratching a match which had already been arranged. The cricket club disbanded during the First World War but in 1922 Colonel W. G. Moore called a meeting to discuss its re-formation. He was himself elected president of the new club, which would share the football club's grounds, then in East Street. Annual subscription was to be five shillings. The new club played its first match in May 1922, against Priory Park. In these early days all cricket matches were away as Selsey had no cricket ground of its own. After the Second World War cricket was resumed in the village under the auspices of the Selsey Evening Institute – at first there was just 'net' practice but between 1946 and 1952 the team managed to play a few matches each season, the home matches held on the playing field of the East Street school. During the 1950s residents began to clamour for improved sports facilities and a local farmer, Mr. Charles Rusbridge, agreed to let the cricket club have the piece of land behind the infants' school, bounded by Paddock Lane and School Lane, for a peppercorn rent. It was to be used for 'cricket and recreation' and was to be maintained by the cricket club 'in perpetuity'. The club played its first home match on its own ground in 1954. At that time the club house was a small old barn, now in the centre of the car park behind the fire station, and the boundary was marked by 100 small triangular flags made by wives of club members. Selsey cricket club won the Local Village Cricket Competition in 1986 and again in 1987.

Selsey had two bowling greens, one at the *Selsey Hotel*, opened in 1912, and one at the side of the *New Inn*, opened the following year by Archibald Hamilton in his capacity as President of Selsey Bowling Club. The Selsey-on-Sea golf club, founded in 1904 by Rowland and Jack Lewis, Maurice and Dick Jewell, and Duncan Berwick, played over an 18-hole course. At the beginning, green fees were 2s. 6d. a day for gentlemen and 1s. 6d. for ladies. The original clubhouse was burnt down in 1933 and the present building opened in July 1934. There were six tennis courts adjacent to the clubhouse. In June 1941 a bomb fell on the golf course, forming a crater round the seventh hole 64 ft. in diameter and 16 ft. deep. Golf continued to be played throughout the war even though only a few holes could be used. Riding was always a popular pastime in Selsey, with residents and holiday makers alike. *Kelly's Directory* for 1930 lists six riding stables in the village, such as the High Street Riding Stables (where the fire station is today) with Mrs. E. R. Mitchell as proprietress. Tennis and bowling have always been played at the Crablands Club off West Street, and in July and August special junior matches and competitions used to be organised for the children during their long school holidays. Other sporting activities in the village today include angling (the club is based at the bottom of Albion Road near the *Lifeboat Inn*) and fishing.

Heated discussions began in the autumn of 1987 as to whether Selsey, whose population has increased fourfold since 1950, should be considered a town rather than a village. This is not a new controversy: in 1902 Selsey considered taking urban status, being the largest village in the area, and as early as 1897 Selsey's tram station was known as the town station. A meeting was called by the Selsey Ratepayers and Residents Association in October 1987.

108. The entrance to Crablands Club, boasting its tennis courts and bowling green. The area has changed little since this photograph was taken in 1949.

An overwhelming majority of those present voted against the adoption of urban status. Most people felt the villagers should resist further development and expansion so that Selsey can retain its unique character and links with the past. This was identical to a decision reported in *The Chichester Observer* in 1975!

Many other leisure activities flourish in the village today, catering for almost all interests however specialised. There has never been any need for the people of Selsey to travel to Chichester to find entertainment. Today the village must have more clubs and societies in relation to its population than almost any other community in the country. In May 1921 a Women's Institute was inaugurated – now there are three separate branches, all very active. Selsey Horticultural Society was founded in 1928 and in its early years held an annual show in the cinema hall. There is also a Royal British Legion Club, meeting in the old Institute building in the High Street, a choral and operatic society, founded in 1962, which has presented many popular musicals of a high standard, and a bridge club, to name but a few. The Selsey Venture Club was founded in 1967 by Mr. Clifford Rhodes. It now owns four minibuses, fully utilised in taking the club's 700 members to shops, the Health Centre, clubs and churches within the village.

It would be wrong to complete this account of leisure activities in Selsey without mentioning the opportunities afforded by Pagham Harbour, which is of nationwide importance to ornithologists. In the 1850s when a report was made on the harbour with a view to possible reclamation, A. E. Knox, an eminent ornithologist, described the various birds to be seen in the harbour at that time – osprey, sandpipers, dotterels, peewit, tern, gulls, oystercatchers, heron, guillemot, divers, pochard and golden-eye ducks were among those mentioned. The variety is remarkable for any single locality and is accounted for by the very southerly position of the peninsula which means that more than 120 migrating species of bird rest at the harbour during the winter months. The mudflats are rich in algae and therefore a good source of food for the birds. In 1988 the harbour was officially classified as a wetland and waterfowl habitat of international importance and was made a Special Protection Area for Birds by the Minister for the Environment. At the end of the 19th century shooting for snipe, wildfowl and geese was a popular sport at Pagham Harbour. It also has interesting salt marsh and shingle beach flora and a distinctive insect population. Selsey folk are fortunate to have a naturalist's haven on their doorstep and many take advantage of the harbour area for walking.

HIGH GROUND DAIRY, SELSEY.

W. JINMAN & SONS,

Dairymen and Cowkeepers.

NEW MILK, FRESH BUTTER, EGGS and POULTRY delivered twice daily.

ALL ORDERS CAREFULLY ATTENDED TO.

A 1910 advertisement.

Postscript

And what of Selsey in years to come? Residents care passionately about the future of their community. This has been proved recently by their united and vociferous opposition to government suggestions that the Manhood peninsula is geologically suitable for the dumping of nuclear waste off shore. Perhaps it is fortunate, in this respect at least, that Selsey is so remote. Even communications with Chichester, a mere eight miles distant, are difficult due to the poor road linking them, so the prohibitive cost of developing the infra-structure needed to transport radioactive waste from nuclear plants to this most southerly part of Sussex means that Selsey is unlikely to be the site ultimately chosen.

However, there are other concerns for the future. Selsey's population structure has changed considerably over the last few decades. The proportion of retired people living in the village has increased from 20 per cent in 1951 to 34 per cent in 1981. Inevitably, there has been a shift at the other end of the age scale, too, with a steady drop in the number of children under 15 years of age. They accounted for 36 per cent of the population in 1971, but today only 15 per cent of Selsey's inhabitants are youngsters. One of the main problems is that there are few employment opportunities in the village. Selsey is rapidly becoming a commuter area, many residents travelling to Chichester and beyond to work each day. The situation could, unfortunately, worsen as two of the traditional employers of labour in the area hit hard times. The tourist trade is in decline, with fewer and fewer people wishing to spend their holidays in caravans by the sea in this country, being lured to more sunny climes by cheap package holidays abroad. This trend has already affected the holiday camps and caravan sites in Selsey. Agriculture is also facing a crisis, with the government encouraging more and more land to be taken out of cultivation and put to other uses. Unless farmland in the Selsey area is profitably re-utilised, employment prospects will become even more restricted. To redress the balance of population, something positive must be done to create work for young people within the village. Also, houses must be built at prices suitable for the first-time buyer, the young married couples so badly needed to safeguard Selsey's future prosperity, who are unable to afford the properties being built at present. On the other hand, there is an understandable fear that house building may get out of hand as permission is given for more and more in-filling, which is rapidly denuding Selsey of its attractive open spaces and distinctive character.

The future is not, however, one of unmitigated gloom. The village certainly faces a challenging time, but Selsey men and women have always felt a strong sense of pride in, and loyalty towards, their community and will undoubtedly work together to preserve what is good from the past and introduce changes which will benefit the entire population as it moves into the 1990s and beyond.

Footnote References

1. By Rev. John Cavis-Brown when he published the map in 1906 (*see* Bibliography).
2. Reid, Clement, *The Geology of the Country around Bognor*, Geol. Survey Mem., 1897, p. 8.
3. *The Chichester Post*, 26 November 1932.
4. F. G. Aldsworth, *The Mound at Church Norton, Selsey, and the Site of St. Wilfrid's Church.*
5. *The Anglo-Saxon Chronicle* give A.D. 477 as the date for Aella's landing, but latest scholarship now considers this to be 20 years out.
6. *See* p. 14 for a discussion of the original dedication of the cathedral.
7. Bond, F. M., *English Cathedrals*, London, 1899.
8. Dr. John Fines, Head of History at the West Sussex Institute of Education, believes that Wilfrid may have sold out the South Saxons to Ceadwalla, attracted by the prospect of increased power. He was given one quarter of the Isle of Wight when the King of Wessex took over Sussex and did not stay long in the area after the conquest, returning to York, perhaps to avoid the wrath of the people of the Selsey peninsula which made up a large proportion of the kingdom of Sussex in those days.
9. Stephens, W. R. W., *Memorials of the South Saxon See and Cathedral Church of Chichester*, 1876.
10. Dallaway, J. and Cartwright, E., *A History of the Western Division of the County of Sussex, including the Rapes of Chichester, Arundel, and Bramber, with the City and Diocese of Chichester*, 1815.
11. Stephens, op. cit.
12. By the time of the Domesday survey the hide was both an area of land, usually 120 acres, and an assessment for tax purposes. The size of a hide varied from county to county and even within counties.
13. Cakam or Cakeham Stone was an area south-west of the present West Wittering and now under the sea. It was to be fortified to protect the entrance to Chichester harbour. The Armada survey did not mention Cakeham Manor, a brick structure built in the 13th century but strengthened with a fortified tower by Bishop Sherburne in 1519 and almost certainly used as a watch tower during the Armada invasion scare.
14. Heron-Allen interpreted the word on the Armada map as dove-houses but John Naish (*see* Bibliography) reads it as 'done-houses', assuming them to be round buildings on promontories, though he admits that the origin of such a word is unknown.
15. *The Gentleman's Magazine*, 1797.
16. Mrs. Vernon-Harcourt later married the Archbishop of York.
17. Wilfrid had been converted from Celtic to Roman Christianity and did not trust his fellow northerners to perform the ceremony in accordance with the rites of Rome.
18. William Cooper, 1858 (*see* Bibliography).
19. The information in this paragraph has been taken from an article by Samuel H. Day printed in *The Chichester Post* in June 1934.
20. Heron-Allen, in quoting from this report in *Selsey Bill: Historic and Prehistoric*, makes the point that the population of the village in 1910 was nearer 1,500 than 1,200.
21. *Daily Telegraph*, 12 May 1934.
22. An alternative theory concerning the name 'Owers' is that it is the last trace of the 'ora' of 'Cymenes ora', the landing place of the South Saxons in 457. Allowing for the constant advance of the sea on the land, it is probable that the Owers lie where the coastline lay in the fifth century. If so, the Owers are the bank on which the ships of the South Saxons first touched shore.
23. Bill House is now a retirement home at the end of Grafton Road. *See* page 116.
24. *The Chichester Post*, June 1932.
25. *Pike's Directory*.
26. The logbook, 1906-37, is now housed in the Record Office in Chichester.
27. Southdown Motor Services Ltd. was formed in June 1915, incorporating the Brighton, Hove and Preston United Omnibus Company, the Worthing Motor Services, and the London and South Coast Haulage Company.

28. *The Chichester Post*, 28 July 1934.
29. Information from 'Civilian War Dead in the United Kingdom, 1939-45', vol. V, courtesy of the Imperial War Museum, London.
30. J. R. A. Peel, of Tillington in Sussex, fired the first shot in the Battle of Britain, on 8 August 1940.
31. In the 1930s H. Pennicott's was situated opposite the Pavilion (cinema hall), between the *Neptune* and N. Wilkins, Butcher. *See* illustrations 56 and 103a.
32. In 1979 the 'Knap stones' were rediscovered, three large granite boulders whose origins are shrouded in mystery, though Heron-Allen mentions them in his book on the village. One was found on the grass area at Large Acres, the housing estate on the site of Heron-Allen's own house of the same name, demolished *c.*1964. Two others were found in the wall along the High Street outside Medmerry School. It is thought that these stones were so named because they used to block the entrance to Knap Lane, adjoining the wall of 'The Homestead'.

Bibliography

Aldsworth, F. G., *The Mound at Church Norton, Selsey, and the Site of St. Wilfrid's Chapel*
Barr-Hamilton, Alec, *In Saxon Sussex*, The Arundel Press
Brunnarius, Martin, *The Windmills of Sussex*, Phillimore, 1979
Busby, Roy, *British Music Hall: An Illustrated Who's Who from 1850 to the Present Day*, Paul Elek Ltd., 1976
Cavis-Brown, Rev. J., *Maps of Selsey, in the County of Sussex, in the Years 1672 and 1901, with Notes on Coast Erosion and Some Features of the Manor*, Chichester, 1906
Colgrave, Bertram (ed.), *The Life of Bishop Wilfrid by Eddius Stephanus*, Cambridge University Press, 1958
Cooper, William, *Smuggling in Sussex*, Frank Graham, 1966 (first published 1858)
Cunliffe, Barry, *The Regni*, Duckworth, 1973
Curwen, E. Cecil, *The Archaeology of Sussex*, Methuen, 1954
Fletcher, Anthony, *Sussex 1600-1660: A County Community in Peace and War*, Phillimore, 1980
Glover, Judith, *The Place Names of Sussex*, Batsford, 1975
Goodwin, John, *The Military Defence of West Sussex*, Middleton Press, 1985
Griffith, Edward, *The Hundred of Manhood and Selsey Tramways*, Herald Press, Farnham, 1968
Haes, E. C. M., *Natural History of Selsey*, Harvester Press, 1977
Hartnoll, Phyllis (ed.), *The Oxford Companion to the Theatre*, Oxford University Press, 1983
Heron-Allen, Edward, *Selsey Bill: Historic and Prehistoric*, Duckworth, 1911
Heron-Allen, Edward, 'Selseyana, 1906-37' (A collection of newspaper cuttings and postcards relating to Selsey, now housed in the West Sussex Record Office.)
Kelly's Directory of Sussex, 1899, 1909, 1918, 1927, 1930, 1934, 1938
Lower, Mark Antony, *The Worthies of Sussex*, 1865
Mawer, A., and Stenton, F. M., *The Place Names of Sussex* Part I, Cambridge University Press, 1929
McDermott, Richard and Richard, *The Standing Windmills of West Sussex*, Richard McDermott Ltd., 1978
Mee, Arthur, *The King's England: Sussex*, Hodder and Stoughton, 1964
Mitchell, Vic, and Smith, Keith, *Branch Line to Selsey*, Middleton Press, 1983
Morris, Colin, *British Bus Systems: Southdown*, The Transport Publishing Co., 1985
Morris, Jeff, *The History of the Selsey Lifeboats*, R.N.L.I. publication, 1986
Morris, John (gen. ed.), *Domesday Book: Sussex*, Phillimore, 1976
Naish, John, *Seamarks, Their History and Development*, Stanford Maritime Ltd., 1985
Page, William (ed.), *The Victoria History of the Counties of England: Sussex*, 1973 (reprinted from the original edition of 1907), vols. I-IV
Prior, Brenda G. J., *A Short History of the Parish Church in Selsey*, Selsey Press Ltd.
Scott, Valerie, and Barty-King, Hugh, *The County Maps and History of Sussex*, Quiller Press Ltd., 1985
Selsey Guide, produced by the Selsey Parish Council
Smith, Arthur C., *Windmills in Sussex: a contemporary survey*, Stevenage Museum publications, 1980
The Southdown Story: A History of Southdown Motor Services Limited, 1915-1965, Southdown Motor Services Ltd., 1965
The Sussex County Magazine, (vol. VI, 1932; vol. IX, 1935; vol. XII, 1938; vol. XVII, 1943; vol. XX, 1946; vol. XXVI, 1952; vol. XXIX, 1955)
Swift, Rowland C., *Methodism in Sussex and its Influence in the Life of the Community, 1756-1900* (published M.Phil. thesis)
Thomas-Stanford, Charles, *Sussex in the Great Civil War and the Interregnum, 1642-1660*, Chiswick Press, 1910
Thurston, Herbert, and Attwater, Donald (eds.), *Butler's Lives of the Saints*, vol. IV, Burns and Oates, 1956
Waugh, Mary, *Smuggling in Kent and Sussex, 1700-1840*, Countryside Books, 1985
White, Miss G. M., 'A Settlement of the South Saxons', in *The Antiquaries Journal*, Oct. 1934
Who's Who in Sussex, 1935
Woodman, Richard, *View from the Sea*, Century Publishing, 1985

Index

Note: numbers in bold type (e.g. **28**) indicate that an illustration of the subject appears on that page.

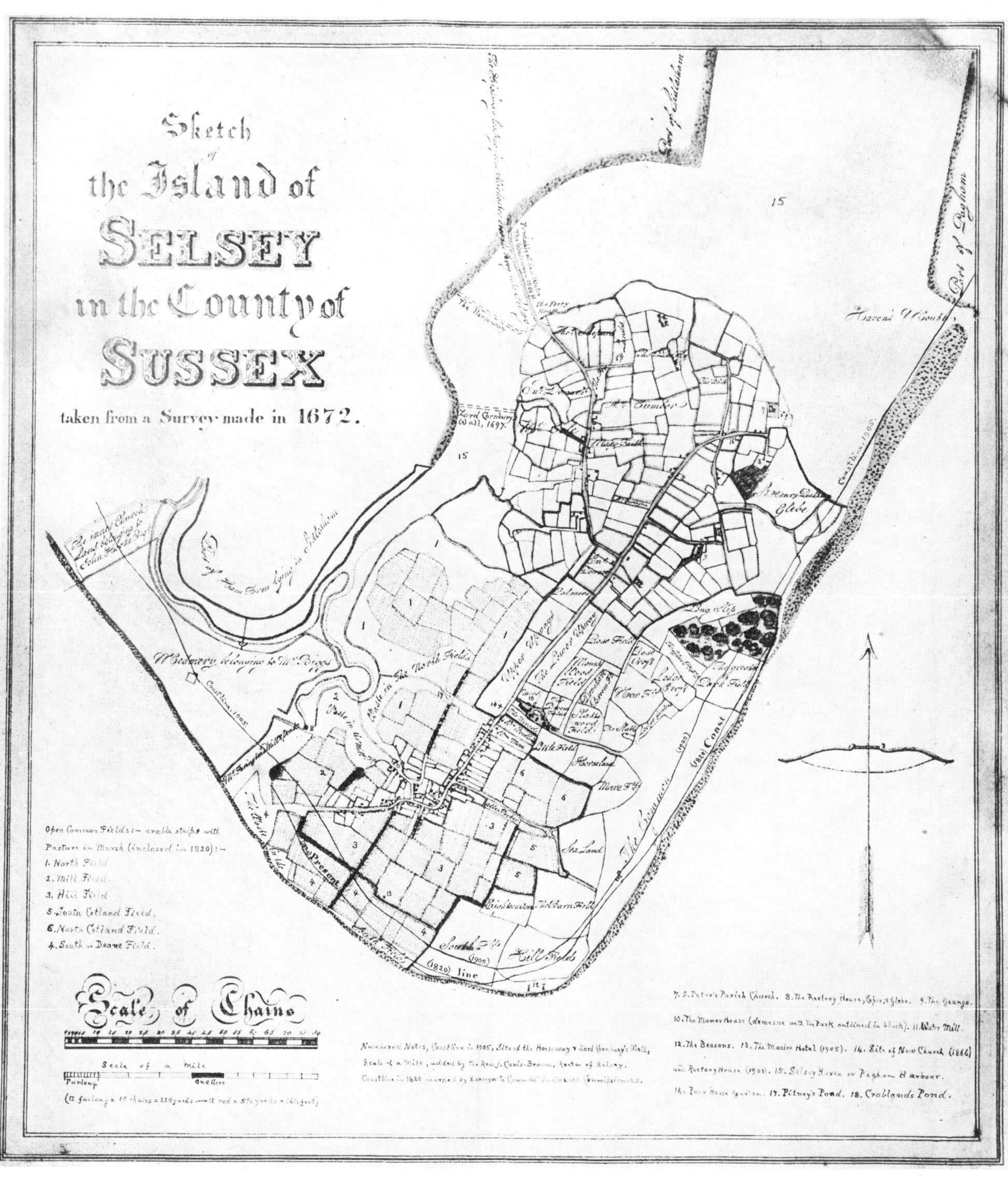

Map of the 'Island' of Selsey drawn in 1672, on which the coastlines of 1820 and 1905 have been added later.